JOHN DONNE

JOHN DONNE

by

K. W. GRANSDEN

REVISED EDITION

ARCHON BOOKS

HAMDEN, CONNECTICUT

1969

FIRST PUBLISHED 1954
REVISED EDITION © 1969 BY K. W. GRANSDEN
THIS EDITION PUBLISHED 1969
BY PERMISSION OF LONGMANS, GREEN & CO. LTD.

SBN: 208 00728 8
LIBRARY OF CONGRESS CATALOG CARD NUMBER: 69 – 18272
PRINTED IN THE UNITED STATES OF AMERICA

PREFACE

I HAVE found the 'Nonesuch' Donne, edited by Mr. John Hayward, to be the best text, since it gives the reader not only all Donne's verse, which he can easily get elsewhere, but also a large selection of the prose (including the whole of *Ignatius His Conclave*) which he cannot easily get elsewhere. For every accessible edition of a prose work by Donne there are three or four of his verse, and in this book, which is offered as a 'companion' to Donne, not as a reassessment of him, I have tried to restore the balance to the extent at least of giving a brief account even of relatively inaccessible works like *Pseudo-martyr*[1] and *Biathanatos*. In quoting from the Sermons, I have kept to the 'Nonesuch' or to Logan Pearsall Smith's selection, since it seemed doubtful if any but specialists would have access to the complete text.[2] Regretfully, I have not given a chapter to the prose letters, though I have quoted several: space does not permit an adequate account nor the letters themselves a sketchy one. Moreover, editions are not easily available:[3] even Gosse's *Life and Letters of John Donne* is out of print and rare. I have also omitted Donne's Latin works.

Throughout, in quoting from the prose works, I have to some extent modernized the seventeenth-century punctuation and typography which, in its original form, might cause difficulty to the ordinary reader to whom the texts themselves may be unfamiliar. But in

[1] We are promised a new edition of this soon.
[2] Vol. I of a new ten-volume edition of all the Sermons, by G. R. Potter and E. M. Simpson, appeared as I was writing this preface.
[3] Mr. I. A. Shapiro is working on the definitive edition.

quoting from the poems, with which more people are familiar, I have retained the original spelling and punctuation. The latter is 'rhetorical' rather than grammatical: that is, it is a guide to the speaking of the verse.[1] The text of the poems which I have used is Grierson's one-volume edition in the Oxford Standard Authors series, the cheapest of the good complete texts.

My debt to modern criticism and scholarship is heavy, and is acknowledged in the footnotes and bibliography, though there will inevitably be omissions. I owe a more personal debt to all those at Cambridge with whom I discussed and by whom I was taught English literature. I also wish to thank Alan Fowles for reading my manuscript and making many corrections and improvements, and my wife for her unfailing help and encouragement throughout.

K. W. G.

[1] For example, an apostrophe is used between two words to signify elision or syncopation.

PREFACE TO THE REVISED EDITION

In reprinting this 'companion' to Donne after fifteen years—during which time much new work has been done on the poet's life and on the text, canon and sources of the poems—I should like to express my thanks to Dr. I. A. Shapiro for giving me a number of corrections in my pages on Donne's career. I have also—within the limits made possible by the process of photographic reproduction—suppressed, added or rewritten a number of phrases and sentences in the critical portion of the book. I have, however, retained my discussion of the twelfth elegy, though this poem has been rejected from the Donne canon by Dame Helen Gardner. I cannot feel as convinced about this as I do about the rejection of the 'Heroical Epistle', my few lines on which I have happily removed. I have, of course, revised the bibliography.

K. W. G.

University of Warwick, 1969

CONTENTS

PART V: PROSE WORKS

ILLUSTRATIONS

. . . The more precise and learned the thought the greater the beauty, the passion; the intricacies and subtleties of his imagination are the length and depths of the furrow made by his passion. His pedantry and his obscenity—the rock and the loam of his Eden—but make me the more certain that one who is but a man like us all has seen God.

W. B. Yeats on Donne, in a letter to Grierson, 1912.

Lord thou hast made us for thy selfe, and our heart cannot rest, till it get to thee.

St. Augustine, as translated by Donne in a sermon preached at St. Paul's Cross, 1629

I. INTRODUCTION

Go through the iron gate into the south choir aisle of St. Paul's Cathedral in London, and you will see, in a niche on the south wall, the effigy and epitaph of John Donne. By a strange chance it is the only one of the many monuments of the old cathedral, of which he was Dean, to have survived the fire of 1666. Only on the urn beneath are faint traces of burning still discernible. The statue itself is of peculiar interest because it was carved from a drawing commissioned by Donne himself as he lay dying in 1631. 'It seems to breathe faintly,' said Donne's friend Sir Henry Wotton[1] when he saw it, 'and posterity shall look upon it as a kind of artificial miracle.' A modern visitor to St. Paul's who knows anything of Donne's life or work may well feel the same fascination that Wotton felt, and recall the wondering question of Leontes before the 'statue' of Hermione in the last scene of *The Winter's Tale*:

> see my lord,
> Would you not dream it breathed and that those
> veins
> Did verily draw blood?

Donne's first biographer was Izaak Walton (1593–1683), author of *The Compleat Angler*, who as a young man

---

[1] Wotton, diplomatist, poet and Provost of Eton, died in 1639. His friendship with Donne began when the two were students at Oxford.

lived in the parish of St. Dunstan's-in-the-West, Fleet
Street, of which Donne was the incumbent during the
last seven years of his life. In his *Life* of Donne, first
published in 1640, Walton has recorded the story of
how the statue was executed.

A monument being resolved upon, Dr. Donne sent for a
carver to make for him in wood the figure of an urn, giving
him directions for the compass and height of it; and to
bring with it a board of the just height of his body. 'These
being got; then without delay a choice painter was got to
be in a readiness to draw his Picture, which was taken as
followeth—Several Charcole-fires being first made in his
large study, he brought with him into that place his winding-
sheet in his hand, and, having put off all his cloathes, had
this sheet put on him, and so tyed with knots at his head and
feet, and his hands placed so, as dead bodies are usually
fitted to be shrowded and put into their coffin, or grave.
Upon this urn he thus stood with his eyes shut, and with
so much of the sheet turned aside as might shew his lean,
pale and death-like face, which was purposely turned towards the East, from whence he expected the second
coming of his and our Saviour Jesus.' In this posture he was
drawn at his just height; and when the picture was fully
finished, he caused it to be set by his bedside, where it
continued and became his hourly object till his death: and
was then given to his dearest friend and executor Doctor
Henry King, then chief Residentiary of St. Paul's, who
caused him to be thus carved in one entire piece of white
marble, as it now stands in that Church; and by Dr. Donne's
own appointment, these words were to be fixed to it as his
epitaph:

JOHANNES DONNE
Sac: Theol: Profess

Post varia stvdia qvibvs ab annis tenerrimis fideliter
nec infeliciter incvbvit instinctv et impvlsv Spir: Scti
Monitv et Hortatv REGIS JACOBI Ordines Sacros

AMPLEXVS ANNO SVI JESV 1614 ET SVAE AETAT 42 DECANATV
HVJVS ECCLES^{AE} INDVTVS 27° NOVEMB: 1621 EXVTVS MORTE
VLTIMO DIE MARTII A° 1631. HIC LICET IN OCCIDVO CINERE
ASPICIT EVM CVJVS NOMEN EST ORIENS

This epitaph may be translated:

> John Donne, theologian. After various studies to which
> from his earliest years he had applied himself faithfully and
> not unsuccessfully, he took holy orders, through the power
> and inspiration of the Holy Ghost and on the advice and
> persuasion of King James, in the year 1614 and the 42nd
> year of his life. On 27 November 1621 he assumed the
> office of Dean of this church; death took it from him on
> the last day of March 1631. Here although in dust that
> passes away, he looks upon Him whose name is Rising.

So ended, or did not end, one of the most remarkable
of English lives. Indeed, nothing in Donne's life so
impressed his contemporaries as his manner of leaving
it, and the strange perpetuation of himself which he
bequeathed. Within a few years of his death the Dean's
fame as a preacher seemed to grow in men's memory,
and his reputation as a poet was extended by the publication of his poems (in 1633), most of them for the first
time. A century later, he had almost ceased to be read.
Today, the poet has once more come into his own, but
the preacher is forgotten or ignored. The truth, of
course, is that like so many remarkable Englishmen of
the Renaissance, Donne was able to make what seems to
us two separate and dissociated reputations, one (among
a few intellectuals and personal friends) as a poet, the
other (among all his contemporaries) as a scholar and
divine. Probably few of those who can now buy his
poems for a few shillings have made the journey to St.
Paul's to see that tangible link with the man who wrote
those poems. Yet the two men are inseparable and the
two lives are one.

2. THE EARLY YEARS

Donne was born in the City of London in 1572. His father (also John) was a prosperous tradesman who became in 1574 Warden of the Company of Ironmongers. His mother Elizabeth[1] was a daughter of the celebrated Tudor dramatist John Heywood. Both his parents were Roman Catholics and in this faith Donne was himself brought up. His mother indeed was descended from a sister of the saint and martyr Sir Thomas More, and her family had long held a conspicuous place among English Catholics. John Heywood was a favourite of Queen Mary during whose reign (1553–8) the English Catholics were able to enjoy a brief spell in the open. For Mary, Heywood composed his poem *The Spider and the Fly*, an allegory in which the Spider, of course, is the Protestant. Heywood's father-in-law William Rastell the lawyer (whose brother John Rastell fell with More) rose to be a judge under Mary, and indeed struggled on in England until 1563, when five years of Elizabethan Protestantism drove him 'underground' to the Continent; but he left behind him a defiant monument to faith and family in his great edition of the *Works of Sir Thomas More* which he printed in 1557. Thus Donne inherited from his mother's family a remarkable tradition both of literary achievement and of religious faith.

The position of English Catholics under Elizabeth I during the twenty years in which Donne grew up is a subject upon which conflicting viewpoints have been expressed by Catholic and non-Catholic historians. Mr. Evelyn Waugh, for example, in his biography of Edmund Campion the Jesuit martyr, speaks of crippling fines and a policy of deliberately pursued hostility.

[1] This remarkable woman survived three husbands and also her son, dying in 1632 a Catholic to the last.

Others have accustomed us to the idea that Catholics were, like minority sects in the early Roman Empire, free to practise their religion, provided that they conformed outwardly to the laws and loyalties of England. There is certainly enough evidence to show that militant and celebrant Catholicism, such as that of necessity practised by an ordained priest of the Roman Church, was severely penalized.

The experiences of the Elizabethan Jesuit Father John Gerard, whose autobiography was recently published from the unique manuscript at Stonyhurst, show that the act of reconciling English people to the Church of Rome was expressly forbidden under penalty of high treason. About 1596 or 1597 Gerard was imprisoned under suspicion of being a papal agent commissioned to seduce the Queen's subjects from their allegiance to her; he subsequently admitted having made converts, and defiantly told his interrogator that he wished he could have made more, 'a hundred thousand and more than that if I could'. 'It would be enough to raise an army against the Queen!' came the alarmed reply. 'The men I should reconcile', said Gerard, 'would be the Queen's men. They would not be against her. We hold that obedience is due to those in authority.'

From the State's point of view, however, Campion and Gerard belonged to a distinct group of 'international' Jesuits trained on the Continent as missionary spies whose task was to enter England in secret and uphold and strengthen the faith of the Catholic inhabitants: it was admittedly subversive in its methods.[1] One martyr did not make a massacre, and because Elizabeth was politically vigilant for attempts from outside England to

[1] The most famous of these continental seminaries supplying ministers to uphold the old faith in Protestant England was that founded at Douai in 1568 by Cardinal Allen.

upset her order and tranquillity, it should not be thought
that she extended her political anxiety to religious
hostility against private Catholic citizens. Donne would
hardly, with his background, have become, as he did at the
age of twenty-six, personal secretary to the Lord Keeper
of the Great Seal of England if this had been the case. It
is clear that Elizabeth was forced, despite her own desire
for a peaceful and tolerant settlement of the Catholic
question, to recognize in organized Continental Catholicism a political danger, which was especially associated
with the Jesuit 'missionaries' (a movement which,
politically, was virtually a fifth column). Pope Pius V
had excommunicated her in 1570, thereby—in theory—
absolving her many Catholic subjects from any religious
allegiance to her. Thereafter, the price of freedom had
to be eternal vigilance. No Catholic could take an
English university degree, and a professed allegiance, even
if strictly non-political, to Rome, was to the talented and
the ambitious Englishman in Elizabeth's time a drawback
at least.

Being Catholics, Donne's parents sent him up to
Oxford early to give him at least the rudiments of a
liberal education before the age of sixteen, when it was
compulsory for students to subscribe to the Thirty-nine
Articles and the Royal supremacy. The young Donne
entered Hart Hall (now Hertford College) in 1584 and
left after six terms. Walton says he then spent three
years at Cambridge, but this has not been established.
In 1591 he settled in London to study law and was
admitted into the Society of Lincoln's Inn in 1592.

The chronology of these early years is somewhat
doubtful. Our primary source of information, Walton's
biography, resembles the 'Lives' of Plutarch in being
an ethical study 'written round' two events—Donne's
conversion and entry into Anglican orders. The early

years are recorded mainly to point an effective moral contrast with the later years, over which Walton's beautiful prose sheds a sad and powerful light of admiration and wonder. The past is best forgotten by being dimly remembered, left as it were in shadow. Indeed, not only was Walton less concerned with the details of Donne's early and obscure years; he was also unlikely to have known much about them. The man he knew and valued was the elderly Dean; as for the fantastic and cynical poet, in so far as he had heard about him he could hardly have understood him, and there is no evidence and small likelihood that Donne spoke easily or often of his youth to the young.

Young men of smallish fortune used at this time to spend a year or two on voluntary military service, in the hope that the expedition for which they chose to enlist would cover itself in glory some of which might redound to themselves. Apart from landing a share in any spoils, the young officer or aide might hope by his wit or grace to bring himself to the notice of the great lord in command of the expedition. Donne was a member of two such expeditions, in 1596 and 1597. The first went to Cadiz to re-singe the King of Spain's beard. It was commanded by Essex and Ralegh, and was a spectacular though somewhat empty success. Drake, Grenville, Hawkins and Frobisher were dead, and with them the golden age of English seamanship. The 1590's had rather a *fin-de-siècle* atmosphere: it was a time of *flâneurs*, memories and disenchantment. Reputations were made too quickly to last, and were tarnished by the unhealthy atmosphere of rebellious strife which produced them. The last years of the great Queen seemed to be decaying with her.

Donne's second expedition was the notorious 'Islands voyage'. Essex was again supreme commander, with

B

Ralegh in charge of the naval squadrons. The two men
quarrelled bitterly, and left accounts of the failure of
the expedition in which they sought their own exonera-
tion. The objects of the expedition were to destroy
the King of Spain's fleet either at sea or in its harbour
at Ferrol, and to capture the Spanish treasure fleet from
the West Indies at the Azores. Essex admits that all his
aims failed but says this was not due to negligence but
because 'the powerful hand of God did bind our hands
and frustrate all our endeavours'. No sooner were they
out of Plymouth when a great storm scattered and
damaged the fleet, and they had to put back again. After
the ships had been repaired, it turned out that all the
food had gone, since they were 'victualled but for three
months'. Then the land army got sick and had to be
discharged, so that the expedition could do no fighting
at Ferrol. At this point, disaster becomes almost farcical.
Ralegh's ship broke its mainyard, Essex's sprung a leak
and his master-carpenter, 'the only skilful man I had',
died before he could mend it. By the time it was mended
the fleet had gone on ahead, and Essex did not catch it
up till it reached Finisterre. Then Ralegh's ship got
lost, and thirty other ships following his lights by night
went off course with him, so a council of war was held
without him. Ferrol was abandoned; and at the Azores
they encountered, not Spanish ships but a deadly calm.
England got little out of the voyage but Donne produced
two striking poems (*The Storme* and *The Calme*) which
were praised by Ben Jonson and are full of remarkable
passages of description. They were addressed as verse-
letters to his friend and fellow law-student Christopher
Brooke, and like most of his verse remained in manuscript till after his death. But it is not so much in the
poems' description as in their application and commentary that Donne's characteristic imagination strikes

out at the reader, forcing him to see in the storm images
and fears that have little to do with wind or rain:

> Some coffin'd in their cabbins lye, equally
> Griev'd that they are not dead, and yet must dye;
> And as sin-burd'ned soules from graves will creepe,
> At the last day, some forth their cabbins peepe:
> And tremblingly' aske what newes, and doe heare so,
> Like jealous husbands, what they would not know.
>
> *The Storme*, 45–50

And it is from the following passage of *The Calme* that
Ben Jonson quoted admiringly long afterwards, to
Drummond at Hawthornden:

> And all our beauty, and our trimme, decayes,
> Like courts removing, or like ended playes.
> The fighting place now seamens ragges supply;
> And all the tackling is a frippery.
> No use of lanthornes; and in one place lay
> Feathers and dust, today and yesterday.
> Earths hollownesses, which the worlds lungs are,
> Have no more winde then[1] the upper valt of aire.
> We can nor lost friends, nor sought foes recover,
> But meteorlike, save that wee move not, hover.
>
> *The Calme*, 13–22

These two poems were among the first to gain for Donne a
reputation among his contemporaries: their steady
popularity is attested in an epigram of Thomas Freeman
dedicated to Donne in 1614 beginning

> Thy *Storme* described hath set thy name afloat,
> Thy *Calme* a gale of famous winde hath got.

During the four years before these adventures, Donne
may have written many of his more 'outrageous' lyrics
as well as his early satires. The latter are, like all satire
from the Roman prototypes of Horace and Juvenal

---

[1] Then=than, as usual in the orthography of the time.

onwards, urban, or rather metropolitan, in spirit and
subject, and suggest that he spent at least part of those
years in London. Walton also says that he went to Italy
and Spain, 'for some years', *after* the Azores expedition.
We know however that in 1597 he entered the service
of Sir Thomas Egerton in London: and since it is Walton's
chronology that we should suspect rather than his facts,
it seems likely that Donne's European travels either
followed immediately upon his university career, or
preceded his departure on the 1596 expedition.[1] Long
afterwards, Donne said that he had more Spanish books
in his library than of any other language, and in
his first satire (written about 1593) he refers to his
library as containing 'giddie fantastique poets of each
land'. He was certainly fonder of foreign literature than
of English and particularly, from his earliest years, an
admirer of Spanish art and learning, which had reached,
about this time, its unearthly, orchid-like flowering in
the mystical writings of St. Theresa and St. John of the
Cross. In the well-known portrait of Donne executed
in 1591 by William Marshall, he has already adopted a
Spanish tag as his motto: 'antes muerto que mudado'
(sooner dead than altered), a piece of *panache* thoroughly
in keeping with his independent nature. It was the
lighter, Protestant Englishman who most readily went
'Italianate' in Elizabeth's time: to Donne, brought up in
a heavy atmosphere and company of 'men of suppressed
and afflicted religion, accustomed to the despite of
death and hungry of an imagined martyrdom' (his own
words, in the Preface to *Biathanatos*) it was Spain, in
spirit Europe's most truly and most passionately Catholic
country, that clearly made the profoundest and most
permanent appeal. No wonder that in these early

[1] See I. A. Shapiro in *T.L.S.* 23 Oct. 1930, *N.Q.* 211 (1966) pp.
246–7.

travels he turned aside from the Holy Land and went instead to Spain, a fact that Walton was at least bound to record disappointedly.

During these years of foreign travel, Donne probably spent with a natural extravagance the patrimony bequeathed him by his father, who died when he was a child. A man of his position would have had to pay to join the Essex expeditions and might not have come home from them richer than he set out. He obviously bought a great many books, and lived in London the life of a gallant and man about town, fond of women, wine, good conversation and expensive company. It hardly needs saying that the writing of such verse as Donne's early pieces, which were circulated in manuscript among friends, was no more a lucrative occupation then than now. The only way to make money as a poet in those days was to be invited to join the circle of some wealthy and noble patron who would present perquisites, hospitality and advancement to a young writer to whom he had once been introduced and attracted, in return for occasional and commissioned verses. But no one who was unknown, no poor student, however brilliant, could attach himself to a patron unless he first obtained some recognizable position in the way of public service. The patron spotted his artist, not in the tavern or the college, but at the secretary's table.

Donne was fortunate, therefore, at this time to attract the attention at Lincoln's Inn of its then most distinguished figure, Sir Thomas Egerton, who in 1596 became Lord Keeper of the Great Seal of England.[1] Egerton was a personal friend of Essex, and may himself have brought Donne to Essex's notice when the Cadiz expedition was planned. At any rate, Egerton thought

[1] He was later created Baron Ellesmere and Viscount Brackley and became, under James I, Lord Chancellor. He died in 1617.

highly enough of Donne's powers and personality to see in him one who could do the State some service, and appointed him in 1597 his chief secretary.

3. MARRIAGE

In 1593 Donne's brother Henry had died in Newgate where he had been imprisoned for harbouring a priest. He was probably the family's last martyr. Donne himself might not as yet have openly renounced the Catholic faith: it would be truer to say that he had quietly dropped it. In his heart he may have still accepted it, may perhaps have despised State Protestantism. But his brain responded to a world where you were judged not by your secret feelings but by your actions, your 'policy'. Egerton would not have employed a man whom he suspected of being subversive. What his new employee wanted was a secular career, and to obtain one he would have to pay the price of outward religious conformity. Not being of the stuff of which martyrs were made, Donne paid the price, and entered what we should now call the civil service.

But he did not stay there very long. The next adventure to record is his marriage, which Walton called 'the remarkable error of his life', presumably because he knew it cost him his job rather than because he disapproved of marriage in general or thought Donne had married beneath him. For the girl he married was of a highly advantageous social position, and, after all, Donne could scarcely have foreseen the opposition he was to encounter, particularly because his outstanding abilities and personality had in a very short time brought him into contact with Egerton's personal friends and relations as an equal rather than as a secretary. 'Nor did his Lordship,' says Walton, 'in this time of Master Donne's attendance upon him, account him to be so much his servant as to forget he was his friend; and to testify it, did always use him with much courtesy, appointing him a place at his own table, to which he esteemed his company and discourse to be a great ornament.' Donne was probably the youngest and most interesting ornament there, and it is most natural that he should have attracted and fascinated Egerton's sixteen-year-old niece Ann More. Her father was Sir George More of Loseley in Surrey: it was his sister who was Egerton's second wife. But Lady Egerton died in 1600 and Ann seems then to have stayed on at York House, probably to look after the Lord Keeper's household. In any case, by about Christmas of the year 1601, More seems to have got wind of the affair between his daughter and Donne, whereupon he removed her, says Walton, 'with much haste; . . . but too late, by reason of some promises which were so interchangeably passed, as never to be violated by either party'. Shortly after this, having contrived in the meantime to meet and to correspond, they were secretly married in the presence of only five persons. The Rev. Samuel Brooke (he was later Master of Trinity, Cambridge) performed the ceremony, and his brother, Christopher, the addressee of *The Storme* and *The Calme*, was a w.tness. For two months the couple managed somehow to keep the news from Sir George; but on 2nd February Donne, realizing that such a secret could hardly be kept indefinitely, and probably desperate for lack of security and money, sent a letter to his father-in-law, contrite but firm, apologetic but self-possessed, and full of a pleading none the less sincere for being so completely articulated. It is so exactly the letter a brilliant, impecunious and self-appointed son-in-law might write in any age, that it is worth quoting in full. It is also characteristic of its author.

Sir—

If a very respective fear of your displeasure and a doubt that my lord (whom I know, out of your worthiness, to love you much) would be so compassionate with you as to add his anger to yours, did not so much increase my sickness as that I cannot stir, I had taken the boldness to have done the office of this letter by waiting upon you myself to have given you truth and clearness of this matter between your daughter and me, and to show you plainly the limits of our fault, by which I know your wisdom will proportion the punishment.

So long since as her being at York House this had foundation, and so much then of promise and contract built upon it as, without violation to conscience, might not be shaken.

At her lying in the town this Parliament I found means to see her twice or thrice. We both knew the obligations that lay upon us, and we adventured equally; and about three weeks before Christmas we married. And as at the doing there were not used above five persons, of which I protest to you by my salvation there was not one that had any dependence or relation to you, so in all the passage of it did I forbear to use any such person who, by furtherance of it might violate any trust or duty towards you.

The reasons why I did not fore-acquaint you with it (to deal with the same plainness I have used) were these:—

I knew my present estate less than fit for her. I knew (yet knew not why) that I stood not right in your opinion. I knew that to have given any intimation of it had been to impossibilitate the whole matter. And then having these honest purposes in our hearts and these fetters in our consciences, methinks we should be pardoned if our fault be but this, that we did not, by fore-revealing of it, consent to our hindrance and torment.

Sir, I acknowledge my fault to be so great, as I dare scarce offer any other prayer to you in mine own behalf than this, to believe this truth—that I neither had dishonest ends nor means. But for her, whom I tender much more than my fortunes or life (else I would I might neither joy in this life nor enjoy the next), I humbly beg of you that she may not, to her danger, feel the terror of your sudden anger.

I know this letter shall find you full of passion; but I know no passion can alter your reason and wisdom, to which I adventure to commend these particulars;—that it is irremediably done, that if you incense my lord, you destroy her and me; that it is easy to give us happiness, and that my endeavours and industry, if it please you to prosper them, may soon make me somewhat worthier of her.

If any take the advantage of your displeasure against me, and fill you with ill thoughts of me, my comfort is that you know that faith and thanks are due to them only that speak when their informations might do good; which now it cannot work towards any party. For my excuse, I can say nothing, except I knew what were said to you.

Sir, I have truly told you this matter, and I humbly beseech you so to deal in it, as the persuasions of Nature, Reason, Wisdom and Christianity shall inform you; and to accept the vows of one whom you may now raise or scatter—which are, that as my love is directed unchangeably upon her, so all my labours shall concur to her contentment, and to show my humble obedience to yourself.

Yours in all duty and humbleness,

J. Donne.

To the Rt. Worshipful Sir George More, Kt.

From my lodging by the Savoy.

2nd February 1601.[1]

The letter was disarming but unsuccessful. More, irate, plunged into York House; Egerton, who, it must be remembered in his favour, was in no position to seem to countenance a scandal, dismissed Donne from his service. In despair, the poet is said by Walton to have indited in a letter to his wife the sad little epigram

John Donne[2]—Ann Donne—undone.

[1] As at this time England had not reformed the calendar and the year consequently still began on 25 March, this would be 1602 by our reckoning.

[2] The name was pronounced *Dun*.

But More's outraged feelings were not yet soothed. A few days later he charged his son-in-law, and the Brooke brothers as accomplices, with conspiring to a violation of the two legal codes (the common law and the canon or Church law), a marriage without the consent of the girl's father being technically a breach of both. The three of them were promptly arrested and confined in separate prisons.

In that long, unsuccessful letter to his father-in-law Donne had written that he did not know why he was unacceptable as Ann's husband. In a later letter, however, he makes it pretty clear that he knew the reasons well enough: they were, the rumours of his past life when he was said to have had mistresses, and the rumour of his being reared in a corrupt religion. There was no reason for More to doubt the truth of either 'rumour', but what is significant is that Donne in his later letter declares both obstacles to have vanished. This gives us Donne's own word for the fact that by the end of Elizabeth's reign he was no longer a practising Roman Catholic. It is unlikely that he was ever a militant and public advocate of that faith—now he is at pains to recant altogether. Of course, he had to pacify Sir George: but no one who was still ardently Catholic would surrender his faith like that, to say nothing of marrying without the blessing of the Roman rite. There can be little doubt that Donne had finally committed himself to search for a secular career within the established limits of his own country's practices. To his hopes of such a career his marriage was an early blow.

It was the Archbishop of Canterbury as head of the Church of England who finally declared the marriage legal, on 27 April 1602. Donne and the Brookes were released from prison, but the public scandal raised by the whole business made it impossible for Egerton to retract the sentence of dismissal he had pronounced at More's angry instigation, so that at the age of thirty, with a young wife to support, Donne was cast out, unemployed, upon a troubled and talent-weary world. More had only, it seems, withdrawn (in the face of the marriage's declared legality and the husband's good will) his active objections. He did not for a long time extend a helping or a hospitable hand, and Ann left home without a dowry. The subsequent fifteen years of their married life give us only a few glimpses of Ann or of Donne as a husband, but these few make it easy to feel that, although Donne, who was to know and fascinate some of the most remarkable and influential women of the age, had possibly married a girl who could do no more than admire the strangeness and brilliance of his mind, this was nevertheless a happy marriage: and Donne might have countered Walton's phrase about the 'remarkable error' (had he lived to read it) with Shakespeare's

> If this be error, and upon me proved,
> I never writ, nor no man ever loved.

At the beginning of his married life Donne was lucky to be offered board and lodging at Pyrford by his wife's cousin Sir Francis Wooley. In this quiet Surrey village, he spent three years of retirement increasing his knowledge, reading widely (chiefly in theology), borrowing books from Sir Robert Cotton, away from the storms and glare of London, where during this time the great Elizabethan age came slowly to its close. Between 1590 and 1602 Donne must have written many of the secular poems we now admire. Jonson said he wrote 'all his best poems ere he was 25': and although we do not know the names of more than two of the poems Jonson meant (i.e. *The Calme* and *The Storme* mentioned above) we know that the *Satires* and at least some of the *Songs and Sonets* were

written during the stormy 1590's. Others of the love
poems in *Songs and Sonets* probably belong to the period
of his courtship and marriage. What cannot be over-
emphasized is that Donne himself published hardly any of
his verse in his lifetime. The great lyrics, and the Holy
Sonnets, for which posterity has glorified him, were
left to posterity to publicize. Here may be perceived
a defence of the biographical method which separates
'the man who suffers from the artist who creates'.
What Donne himself really thought of his secular verses
we do not know: but as a young man he presumably
thought as highly of them as every young man does of
his verses, and circulated them in manuscript among
friends with careless pride. As an old man, Walton
tells us, 'in his penitential years, viewing some of the
pieces that had been loosely (God knows too loosely)
scattered in his youth, he wish't they had been abortive'.
In those days theology was Queen of the sciences and arts,
the apex to which all lesser knowledge and all other arts
led up, like a ladder of bright angels, to the throne and
source of knowledge: and a man of Donne's temper
and theological strength may certainly in later years
have come to attach what our view may find a startlingly
small importance to the fashionable outpourings of his
'fantastic' days. In the first decade of the new century
Donne was still a man in search of a professional career,
of that outward preferment which is the favour of the
state. Our modern concept of the poet romantically
giving up all thrones and powers for the expression of
his imaginative and creative vision, the lonely adventurer
of the spirit, dates back only to Wordsworth. The
Renaissance, seventeenth- and eighteenth-century poets,
Shakespeare, Dryden, Pope, were in their widely
differing ways professional men putting their sole or
their best talent at the service of society for the highest

returns, not just of fame or 'grace', but of cash, position and power. Donne's 'metaphysical' fancies and gifts were not the kind to keep him in lifelong or satisfactory employment. He could not write verse for the stage nor for the masses: them he was to reach another and more effective way. So there is no reason to see his poetry in relation to his whole early life as more than one facet or expression of his many-sided genius thrusting aside, as it were, in poem after poem, minor discoveries, minor irritations, minor experiments, minor joys, on the way to a fuller self-expression such as could only come through some acknowledged professional position.

But that was, for a time, still to elude him. As he himself realized, and said in a letter to Egerton written after his dismissal, 'To seek preferment here with any but your Lordship were a madness. Every great man to whom I shall address my suit will silently dispute the case, and say "Would my Lord Keeper so disgraciously have imprisoned him and flung him away if he had not done some other great fault of which we hear not?"' This was an ingenious and, doubtless, justified appeal, and even Sir George More apparently wished he had not been so hasty (perhaps he realized that his haste had cost his son-in-law his job and thereby his daughter a home of her own); but Egerton said that 'though he was unfeignedly sorry for what he had done, it was yet inconsistent with his place and credit to discharge and readmit servants at the request of passionate petitioners'. Meanwhile, Pyrford and preferment were just as far apart as Pyrford and London. Then, in 1607, having now two children, Donne moved to Mitcham, nearer the capital. It seems to have been a case of following rather than searching for employment, for the next few years were active ones.

4. THE MIDDLE YEARS

Under James I, who succeeded Elizabeth in 1603, the policy of English Catholics changed for a time from opposition to co-operation. They hoped that, now their arch-enemy, Europe's most formidable Protestant sovereign, was dead, they might find more sympathetic treatment at the hands of her successor. At first indeed James was inclined to reciprocate with a policy of tolerance. But his chief minister, Robert Cecil, Earl of Salisbury, did his best to persuade him to pursue the Elizabethan policy of regarding the Catholics as the party of potential revolution and insurrection, and in fact James was quickly obliged to assume to the full the responsibilities of Defender of the Faith; for in the early years of his reign the Gunpowder Plot was prepared, the object of which was to destroy the English Parliament as the place from which had sprung all the oppressive measures against English Catholics. The attempt to deliver England from 'servitude' failed on 5 November 1605, and as a result severe penalties were imposed on all Catholics. Anti-Catholic propaganda in the form of manifestos and pamphlets began to flood London and the country. This was the work upon which Donne was engaged at Mitcham. It was public service at any rate, if not precisely a secular career. His preference had obviously been to make his living from the law, but his dismissal from Egerton's service made that unlikely. Now, perhaps half-unwillingly, he put his equally great learning in theology at the service of the State.

His qualifications for the work were unquestionable. His polemical prose, all of which was written in the next few years, is ample evidence of his theological knowledge; while, as his own mind held its balance between religion and secularism, he was still, as it were, a free-lance: not by any means mentally indifferent to the war between Catholic and Protestant—for he was a keen controversialist; and not by any means disposed to regard it as unimportant; an enthusiastic umpire, a lover of the game to such an extent as to regard it as much more than a game, but not committed emotionally, as yet, to either side. One last qualification would not have been overlooked; Donne had been born a Catholic, but had not since early youth evinced any signs of deep attachment to Catholicism. Who better could make war on Rome than one who had been born, but had not confirmed himself, her servant, who had inherited her learning and her outlook but had escaped from her prejudices?

The chief organizer of the campaign was Thomas Morton, who in 1607 became Dean of Gloucester and eventually Bishop of Durham.[1] It was in 1607 that Morton made a bid to get Donne into the Church of England. It was a failure: a greater than Morton was needed to bring Donne, his eyes still half-averted to the glittering secular world, into a religious career. He was never (from the time of his maturity and marriage onward) without great spiritual aptitude. But he was also endowed with great temporal skills, and was not yet, at the age of thirty-five, prepared to surrender all chance of temporal eminence. Many years later, Izaak Walton got the story of Morton's attempt to convert Donne from the aged Bishop himself, and tells it in his *Life of Donne* as follows:—

> He [Morton] sent to Mr. Donne, and intreated to borrow an hour of his time for a conference the next day. After their meeting, there was not many minutes passed

[1] He was one of the King's chaplains, and though seven years Donne's senior survived him by nearly thirty years.

before he spake to Mr. Donne to this purpose: 'Mr. Donne, the occasion of sending for you is to propose to you what I have often revolved in my own thought since I last saw you: which nevertheless, I will not declare but upon this condition, that you shall not return me a present answer, but forbear three days, and bestow some part of that time in Fasting and Prayer; and after a serious consideration of what I shall propose; then return to me with your answer. Deny me not, Mr. Donne: for it is the effect of a true love, which I would gladly pay as a debt due for yours to me.' This request being granted, the Doctor expressed himself thus: 'Mr. Donne, I know your education and abilities: I know your expectation of a state employment, and I know your fitness for it; and I know too, the many delays and contingencies that attend Court-promises; and let me tell you that my love begot by our long friendship, and your merits, hath prompted me to such an inquisition after your present temporal estate, as makes me no stranger to your necessities, which I know to be such as your generous spirit could not bear, if it were not supported with a pious patience: you know I have formerly persuaded you to waive your court-hopes and enter into Holy Orders; which I now again persuade you to embrace with this reason added to my former request: the King hath yesterday made me Dean of Gloucester and I am also possessed of a benefice, the profits of which are equal to those of my Deanry; I will think my Deanry enough for my maintenance (who am and resolved to die a single man) and will quit my benefice and estate you in it, (which the patron is willing I shall do) if God shall incline your heart to embrace this motion. Remember, Mr. Donne, no man's education or Parts make him too good for this employment, which is to be an Ambassador for the God of Glory, that God who by a vile death opened the gates of life to mankind.'

In intimating that he knew Donne was in need of regular employment, Morton shrewdly showed he knew what he was at: and in the moving and noble closing

phrases of exhortation, any student of the English language and of this present situation will see a peculiar
felicity in the choice of the word Ambassador (whether
Morton's in original fact or only in subsequent recollection: the record seems to be that of a conversation
Morton was unlikely to have forgotten any word of).
With no lack of sincerity in this manifestation of that
spirit of compromise between this world and the next
which is so very English and hence so very Anglican,
he just hints that the Church can overbid the State's
call: hints, too, at the bird in hand . . .

Walton continues:

At the hearing of this, Mr. Donne's faint breath and per-
plext countenance gave a visible testimony of an inward
conflict. But he performed his promise, and departed without returning an answer till the third day, and then his
answer was to this effect:

'My most worthy and most dear friend, since I saw you,
I have been faithful to my promise, and have also meditated
much of your great kindness, which hath been such as
would exceed even my gratitude: but that it cannot do;
and more I cannot return you; and I do that with an heart
full of humility and thanks, though I may not accept of your
offer. But, Sir, my refusal is not for that I think myself
too good for that calling,—for which Kings, if they think
so, are not good enough; nor for that my education and
learning, though not eminent may not, being assisted with
God's grace and humility, render me in some measure fit
for it: but I dare make so dear a friend as you are my Con-
fessor; some irregularities of my life have been so visible
to some men, that though I have, I thank God, made my
peace with him by penitential resolutions against them,
and by the assistance of his Grace banished them my
affections; yet this, which God knows to be so, is not so
visible to men as to free me from their censures, and it
may be, that sacred calling from a dishonour. And besides,
whereas it is determined by the best of Casuists that God's

C

glory should be the first end, and a maintenance the second motive to embrace that calling; and though each man may propose to himself both together, yet the first may not be put last without a violation of conscience, which he that searches the heart will judge. And truly my present condition is such, that if I ask my own conscience, whether it be reconcileable to that rule, it is at this time so perplexed about it, that I can neither give myself nor you an answer. You know, Sir, who says *Happy is that man whose conscience does not accuse him for that thing which he does*. To these I might add other reasons that dissuade me, but I crave your favour that I may forbear to express them, and, thankfully, decline your offer.'

Partly, no doubt, Donne was still holding out in the hope of secular preferment; partly, he was still genuinely undecided about his personal religious views. From Rome he had long since escaped, and does not mention it in the reply to Morton, unless it is one of the 'irregularities of my life' or one of the 'other reasons that dissuade me' alluded to at the end of the reply but not disclosed. But was he any nearer to Canterbury? Walton declares that he was still not sure, and there is no reason to doubt the substance of Walton's record on so important a point. The impression of reluctance to commit himself which he gives is characteristic of Donne. Walton's comment is slightly dramatic: 'This was his present resolution. But the heart of man is not in his own keeping.'

The reply to Morton also contains a cautious reference to the more practical side of his offer. Until he was nearly forty, Donne was constantly short of money. A man of great independence of character and no little emotional and intellectual pride, he was forced by circumstance to conceal his pride and to be an employee. But the various odd jobs, literary, legal, theological, from the time of his first service with Egerton down to his ordination nearly twenty years later, were all such as enabled him to keep his independence of conscience and his freedom of mind and spirit. He could still remain 'uncommitted', even though—perhaps because—that meant being perplexed, being unable to give himself or any other man an answer. To accept a salary from the Church of England would require a profounder *engagement*, which he was not yet able to see his way clear to making. The offer of 'maintenance' must have tempted him at this time, but he was ready to resist it. This quality of self-sufficiency and independence is visible in many passages of Donne's personal writings. Here is one such passage, from a verse-letter addressed to his lifelong friend Sir Henry Wotton:

> Be thou thine owne home, and in thy selfe dwell;
> Inne any where, continuance maketh hell.
> And seeing the snaile, which every where doth rome,
> Carrying his owne house still, still is at home,
> Follow (for he is easie pac'd) this snaile,
> Bee thine owne Palace, or the world's thy gaile.
> And in the worlds sea, do not like corke sleepe
> Upon the waters face; nor in the deepe
> Sinke like a lead without a line: but as
> Fishes glide, leaving no print where they passe,
> Nor making sound; so closely thy course goe,
> Let men dispute, whether thou breathe, or no.

So Donne remained in the world: but neither his temperament (always passionate and tending to morbid ups and downs of extreme clarity and grasp and extreme despair) nor his financial circumstances, made him happy in it. In his letters during his time at Mitcham, *res angusta domi* crops up time and again, in such ironic codicils as 'dated from my prison at Mitcham', 'my hospital', etc. For he was sick as well as poor, and in 1608 seriously ill. In that year, when life at Mitcham seems to have reached a climax of struggle and misery,

he wrote a treatise called *Biathanatos*, in defence of
suicide, the preface to which contains these words:
'Whensoever any affliction assails me, methinks I have
the keys of my prison in mine own hand, and no remedy
presents itself so soon to my heart as mine own sword.'
(Needless to say this work was among those unpublished
till after his death.) And in a letter written some years
later, he reiterates that 'I had the same desire of death
when I went with the tyde and enjoyed fairer hopes
than now'. He reproaches himself, at Mitcham, for
time spent on restless private study still undisciplined
by any official or directed purpose: in this love of
learning ('the worst voluptuousness', he calls it) he is
like a Faustus who, after long temptation and disappointment, with more wisdom and more humility than
Marlowe's Faustus, will make his pact not with the
Devil but with God. And in his despair we hear the
voice of the Elizabethan *fin-de-siècle* and of an era more
slow to die even than its queen. 'I fear', writes Donne,
'that my present discontent does not proceed from a
good root, that I am so well content to be nothing, that
is, dead. But, Sir, my Fortune hath made me such as I
am rather a sickness or disease of this world than any
part of it, and therefore neither love it nor life.' We
see here something of that bitter preoccupation with
nothingness that marks so deeply the spirit of this age
of *Hamlet* and *King Lear*: it is an age of shadows, things
which are not. Perhaps the best way to understand
Donne's feeling about Fortune at this time (by which
he meant of course the Court in London, supreme em-
ployer which could make or break the gifted) is to
read the plays of his contemporary Webster, which
melodramatize the corrupting power of the Court to
undo those whose gifts, by the nature of the times,
impel them to stake all on shining there. Donne

himself, years afterwards, could illustrate a point in a sermon by saying, 'If I had fixt a son in Court, I were satisfied for that son'. For Donne, the artistic fruit, the climax of these dark and unhappy years, is the pair of long poems, *The Anniversaries*, of 1611–12. There he exorcises his *contemptus mundi* by balancing it, splendidly, with praise of heaven. Also, in the years 1607–9, he may have written some of those passionate, sombre and extremely personal Holy Sonnets, the ones containing references to a ruined life wasting away, to imminent death, to sickness, to failure and to despair.

> Thou hast made me, And shall thy worke decay?
> Repaire me now, for now mine end doth haste,
> I runne to death, and death meets me as fast,
> And all my pleasures are like yesterday;
> I dare not move my dimme eyes any way,
> Despaire behind, and death before doth cast
> Such terrour, and my feeble flesh doth waste. . . .

These years may be taken as the nadir of Donne's fortunes, both temporal and spiritual. Perhaps indeed, as regards the latter, the offer of Morton, though refused, gave Donne fresh reason to think out his religious problems, to try if he could one day make his conscience 'reconcileable to that rule' which could alone give him a career that was both secular and religious. Meanwhile, early in 1609, there came at last a material improvement in the shape of a belated dowry from Sir George More for his daughter. It was Sir Francis Wooley who finally persuaded Sir George into 'conditioning by bond to pay Mr. Donne 800 L. at a certain day, as portion with his wife, or 20 L. quarterly for their maintenance as the interest of it, till the said portion was paid' (Walton). The pound was probably worth in James I's reign about fifteen times what it is now, so that this dowry meant a regular annual income of about £1200 a year. It probably came, for Donne, in the nick of time: but now, even allowing for debts he might have had to pay off, he was free from serious financial worry.

Yet there was a happier side to the Mitcham years. Donne had a gift for friendship, and knew well many of the people who most mattered outside the narrow and exalted circle of the Court itself. Among his friendships at this time it is pleasant and important to note one in particular: his association with the Herbert family, and especially with Magdalen Herbert, *née* Newport. Of this remarkable woman her eldest son Edward (Lord Herbert of Cherbury), who shared with Donne the friendship and esteem of Ben Jonson, wrote in his auto-biography that 'she lived most virtuously and lovingly with her husband for many years . . . and briefly was that woman Dr. Donne hath described in his funeral sermon of her printed'. Another her sons was George Herbert, like Donne a poet and divine, and like Donne the subject of a biography by Izaak Walton. In that work Walton tells of the friendship between Donne and Lady Herbert, and prints a graceful letter addressed to her by him in 1607, beginning 'Your favours to me are everywhere; I use them and have them. I enjoy them at London, and leave them there; and yet I find them at Mitcham.' The letter was accompanied by some 'holy hymns and sonnets', possibly the cycle of seven known as 'La Corona'. Donne dismisses them in the letter by saying that they 'for the matter not the workmanship have escaped the fire'. They are among his earliest religious writings.

It was probably about this time, too, that Donne wrote for Lady Herbert the lovely elegy *The Autumnall*, where, he says, 'affection takes reverence's name'. The poem is not dated, though a manuscript copy of it

exists dated 1620 so it must have been written before
that, and not, as Gosse thought, about 1625. But women
in Donne's day (and men too) would seem old at fifty,
and middle-aged at thirty-five. It is the period between
these ages that we should expect Donne to call 'autumnall'. He expressly repudiates, after all, in this elegy,
any affection for extreme old age—

> But name not *Winter-faces*, whose skin's slacke,
> Lanke, as an unthrifts purse; but a soules sacke;
> Whose *Eyes* seeke light within, for all here's shade;
> Whose *mouthes* are holes, rather worne out, then made.

Lady Herbert was at least forty in 1607, when we first
find Donne in regular correspondence with her. *The
Autumnall* is a characteristic metaphysical poem of Donne's
'middle period,' thoroughly secular in style: in its wit
and its tenderness it is a *fashionable* poem, such as one
could not imagine Donne writing in his last years; the
idea implicit in 'not panting after growing beauties'
seems inconsistent with the grave Dean 'crucified to
the world'.

> I hate extreames; yet I had rather stay
> With *Tombs*, then *Cradles*, to weare out a day.
> Since such loves naturall lation[1] is, may still
> My love descend, and journey downe the hill,
> Not panting after growing beauties, so,
> I shall ebbe out with them, who home-ward goe.

Tenderness is not normally a quality attributed to
Donne, but the last line of *The Autumnall* is as tender as
it is civilized.

Besides Magdalen Herbert, an even greater lady was
among Donne's friends at this time, his patroness Lucy,
Countess of Bedford. Many are the poems addressed
and dedicated to her, and many the poets whom she

---

[1] i.e. motion: a technical term used in astrology.

favoured and drew down to Twickenham where she
lived. Such poets in attendance upon the courts of the
great would be expected to provide occasional verses
for marriages, funerals, etc., within the household.
One of Donne's most impressive performances in this
kind is the elegy he wrote for the death of Bridget Lady
Markham, Lucy's cousin, who died, apparently by
drowning, at Twickenham on 4 May 1609. Her virtues
were also celebrated in melodious verse by Francis
Beaumont, but Donne's elegy is neither graceful nor
complaisant. And as it belongs among those 'occasional'
poems with which Donne must have earned his reputation
for wit and learning, and which are often overlooked in
favour of the love-lyrics which he wrote to please himself,
an excerpt may suitably be given here. The poem is in
every respect characteristic of his poetic genius in its
middle years: that period of considerable literary activity
which followed the lightening of the burden of his financial troubles.

Man is the World, and death th' Ocean,
To which God gives the lower parts of man.
This Sea invirons all, and though as yet
God hath set markes and bounds, twixt us and it,
Yet doth it rore, and gnaw, and still pretend,[1]
And breaks our bankes, when ere it takes a friend.
Then our land waters (teares of passion) vent;
Our waters, then, above our firmament,
(Teares which our Soule doth for her sins let fall)
Take all a brackish tast and Funerall,
And even those teares, which should wash sin, are sin.
We, after Gods *Noe*,[2] drowne our world againe.
Nothing but man of all invenom'd things
Doth worke upon itselfe, with inborne stings.
Teares are false Spectacles, we cannot see

[1] Encroach upon the land, man's kingdom.
[2] God's work of redemption, making despair unnecessary.

Through passions mist, what wee are, or what shee.[1]
In her this sea of death hath made no breach,
But as the tide doth washe the slimie beach,
And leaves embroder'd workes upon the sand,
So is her flesh refin'd by deaths cold hand.
As men of China, after an ages stay,
Do take up Porcelaine, where they buried Clay;
So at this grave, her limbecke, which refines
The Diamonds, Rubies, Saphires, Pearles, and Mines,
Of which this flesh was, her soule shall inspire
Flesh of such stuffe, as God, when his last fire
Annuls this world, to recompense it, shall,
Make and name then, th' Elixar of this All.

For another patron Donne wrote, shortly afterwards,
two longer and more celebrated elegies. In 1610 the
daughter and sole heir of Sir Robert Drury, of Hawstead
in Suffolk, died at the age of fifteen. Donne took the
particular event, as usual, as an opportunity to write
about the place and meaning of death in the Christian
universe, and the two *Anniversaries*, containing between
them about a thousand lines, offer some of his richest reflections on the eternal questions of mortality. They were
almost the only poems of his which were printed during
his lifetime; anonymously, it is true, but his authorship
by that time could not, and did not, fail to be recognized.
Although the poems contain some of the finest work
Donne ever did, astonishing in their sheer brilliance,
crowded with memorable incidental passages full of
originality and truth, they did not seem like that to contemporaries. Ben Jonson told William Drummond that
'Donne's *Anniversary* was profane and full of blasphemies,
that he told Mr. Donne, if it had been written of the
Virgin Mary it had been something; which he answered
that he described the idea of a woman and not as she was'.
In a letter to a friend, George Gerrard, written from

---

[1] The subject of the elegy.

Paris in 1612, Donne himself offers further interesting comments on the poems:

> Of my *Anniversaries*, the fault which I acknowledge in myself is to have descended to print anything in verse, which though it have excuse, even in our times, by example of men, which one would think should as little have done it, as I; yet I confess I wonder how I declined to it, and do not pardon myself. But for the other part of the imputation of having said so much, my defence is, that my purpose was to say as well as I could; for since I never saw the gentlewoman I cannot be understood to have bound myself to have spoken just truth; but I would not be thought to have gone about to praise anybody in rhyme, except that I took such a poem, as might be capable of all that I could say.

Donne makes it pretty clear in this letter how he regarded the 'profession' of poetry. The rest of his defence is against the charge of hyperbole: that a mere mortal girl should become the excuse and subject for such metaphysical extravagances and speculations. Donne's original intention, declared in the *Second Anniversary*, lines 35–6, of inditing a similar poem upon every successive anniversary of the unfortunate young lady's death, was never carried out: Sir Robert probably indicated that enough was for his purposes as good as a feast. The poems are examples of metaphysical verse in its grandest manner. They may not have been an unqualified success with everyone who read them; but their composition led Donne to a closer association with Sir Robert Drury, who must have been impressed, if a little overwhelmed, when 'one fair daughter and no more, the which he loved passing well' was thus heaped with the transcendental honours of this remarkable man's ingenuity.

We know that Donne had already, in 1601, become attached to Sir Robert, who besides being lord of the manor of Hawsted owned a large house in Drury Lane, Westminster, where an apartment, rent-free, was at Donne's disposal. Thus Donne succeeded in creeping once more into the heart of the London he loved, and from which he had been exiled for nearly ten years; for to a true Londoner Mitcham is as much a Tomi as if it were Tomi itself. Was it perhaps partly love of London that prevented Donne from being attracted to Morton's offer of a living, a country living? Was it despair of ever belonging to London, being an official part of it, not a mere satellite or hanger-on, that caused Donne in 1609 to fish (in vain) for a post in the new wild-west commonwealth of Virginia? But he was nearly forty now, and must have felt that he was not likely, nor inclined, to go far away from London again.

He did, however, go more than once to Europe, though he never saw the new world:

> O my America! my new-found-land

—that wonderful conceit remained, for Donne, a conceit from the country of the mind. Instead, about Christmas 1611, he accompanied Drury on a visit to the Continent. Walton says they went as part of Lord Hay's embassy 'to the then French King, Henry IV': but Henry had been assassinated in May of the previous year, and Hay undertook no diplomatic mission at this time. It seems more likely that this was primarily a private tour. We know they went to Amiens and Paris, and were in Frankfurt for the crowning of the Emperor Matthias in June 1612.[1]

As for Donne, he seems to have set out in a melancholic frame of mind; the following passage from a letter gives one the impression that its author is profoundly

[1] In a letter preserved at the British Museum, Drury writes home from Frankfurt a few days after this coronation, referring with some condescension to the junketings of the German princes (Cotton MS. Julius C. III, f. 159).

conscious of being near a climacteric in his life's pilgrimage.

> I am near the execution of that purpose for France; though I may have other ends, yet if it do but keep me awake it recompenses me well. I am now in the afternoon of my life, and then it is unwholesome to sleep. It is ill to look back, or give over in a course; but worse never to set out.

Forty was the afternoon of an Elizabethan's life: the very phrase is thoroughly Elizabethan; his expectation was far less than ours, and it was, besides, fashionable to grow old early. This fashion was revived by Mr. T. S. Eliot in *Prufrock*, written when the poet was under thirty:

> I grow old . . . I grow old . . .
> I shall wear the bottoms of my trousers rolled—

A similar disposition to dwell on age, death, and the 'afternoon' or 'autumn' of life runs through Shakespeare's sonnets, which are also the work of a man whom we should call young. It is extraordinary, also, how powerfully Donne's whole personality tolls like a bell in the undertones of a private letter; not written as measured public prose, it nevertheless has the same quality and effect as many a passage from his later prose writings. The plain syntax of the short sentences emphasizes the sense of fatalistic restlessness.

Before leaving on this visit, which seems to have lasted about ten months, Donne is said by Walton to have written his wife that very moving poem (later included in the *Songs and Sonets*), *A Valediction: forbidding mourning*: and he also gave her the *Song* beginning 'Sweetest love, I do not goe', which contains one of his most famous metaphysical conceits—the souls of true lovers as a pair of compasses, united even in absence unlike the 'sublunary' lovers of Petrarchan convention:

As virtuous men passe mildly away,
   And whisper to their soules, to goe,
Whilst some of their sad friends doe say,
   The breath goes now, and some say, no:

So let us melt, and make no noise,
   No teare-floods, nor sigh-tempests move,
T'were prophanation of our joyes
   To tell the layetie our love.

Moving of th' earth brings harmes and feares,
   Men reckon what it did and meant,
But trepidation of the spheares,
   Though greater farre, is innocent.

Dull sublunary lovers love
   (Whose soule is sense) cannot admit
Absence, because it doth remove
   Those things which elemented it.

But we by a love, so much refin'd
   That our selves know not what it is,
Inter-assured of the mind,
   Care lesse eyes, lips, and hands to misse.

Our two soules therefore, which are one,
   Though I must goe, endure not yet
A breach, but an expansion,
   Like gold to ayery thinnesse beate.

If they be two, they are two so
   As stiffe twin compasses are two,
Thy soule the fixt foot, makes no show
   To move, but doth if the other doe.

And though it in the center sit,
   Yet when the other far doth rome,
It leanes, and hearkens after it,
   And grows erect, as that comes home.

> Such wilt thou be to mee, who must
>   Like th' other foot, obliquely runne;
> Thy firmnes makes my circle just,
>   And makes me end, where I begunne.

In January 1612, while her husband was on the
Continent, Ann was delivered of her eighth child, which
died at birth. The following remarkable incident of
telepathy is recorded by Walton in his *Life*:

At the time of Mr. Donne's and his wife's living in Sir
Robert's house, the Lord Hay was by King James sent upon
a glorious Embassy to the then French King Henry the
Fourth, and, Sir Robert put on a sudden resolution to
accompany him to the French court, and to be present at
his audience there. And, Sir Robert put on as sudden a
resolution to solicit Mr. Donne to be his companion in
that journey: and this desire was suddenly made known to
his wife, who was then with child, and otherways under so
dangerous a habit of body as to her health, that she profest
an unwillingness to allow him any absence from her; saying,
her divining soul boded her some ill in his absence; and
therefore, desired him not to leave her. This made Mr.
Donne lay aside all thoughts of the journey and really to
resolve against it. But Sir Robert became restless in his
persuasion for it; and, Mr. Donne was so generous as to
think he had sold his liberty when he received so many
charitable kindnesses from him, and told his wife so; who
did therefore with an unwilling-willingness give a faint
consent to the journey, which was proposed to be but for
two months: for about that time they determined to return.
Within a few days after this resolve, the Ambassador,
Sir Robert, and Mr. Donne, left London; and were the
twelfth day got safe to Paris—two days after their arrival
there, Mr. Donne was left alone, in that room in which
Sir Robert and he and some other friends had dined together. To this place Sir Robert returned within half an
hour; and, as he left, so he found Mr. Donne alone; but
in such an Extasie, and so altered in his looks, as amaz'd

Sir Robert to behold him: insomuch that he earnestly desired Mr. Donne to declare what had befallen him in the short time of his absence? to which Mr. Donne was not able to make a present answer: but after a long and perplexed pause did at last say 'I have seen a dreadful vision since I saw you: I have seen my dear wife pass twice by me through this room, with her hair hanging about her shoulders, and a dead child in her arms: this I have seen since I saw you.'

It later turned out, says Walton, that 'the abortion prov'd to be the same day, and about the very hour' of Donne's vision.

It is perhaps of interest that in the above account Ann is made to say, in trying to prevent her husband from leaving her to go abroad, that 'her divining soul boded her some ill'. A similar phrase was used by Donne himself in one of the loveliest of his *Songs and Sonets*, the song written at this time for his wife and beginning 'Sweetest love, I do not goe'. In the last verse he gently tries to set aside her fears:

> Let not thy divining heart
>   Forethinke me any ill,
> Destiny may take thy part
>   And may thy feares fulfill;
>   But thinke that wee
> Are but turned aside to sleepe;
> They who one another keepe
>   Alive, ne'r parted bee.

Walton must have been thinking of these lines as he wrote.

5. ORDINATION

About the time of his return to England in the autumn of 1612, Donne seems to have made a fresh effort to think out his position. Despite his wife's dowry, he must have been anxious about the future. He was past forty, and had now a considerable family to support. His own tastes were civilized, and book-buying, in which he indulged fairly extensively, was not cheap. Still greater must have been his psychological need for professional security. The capricious goodwill of patrons, even generous and enlightened ones like Lucy Russell, was a precarious substitute for the independence he needed. If he failed to get it, all he would have to look forward to would be, in the words of another disappointed suitor, John Lyly, to Queen Elizabeth, the bequeathing of three legacies, 'patience to my creditors, melancholy without measure to my friends, and beggary without shame to my family'.

According to Walton, 'many persons of worth mediated with his Majesty for some secular employment for him . . . and particularly the Earl of Somerset'. But no such employment was forthcoming. In 1613, Donne sent, *via* Lord Hay, the following letter to Somerset (the King's first minister), asking for a post in the Church of England:

My Lord—I may justly fear that your Lordship has never heard of the name which lies at the bottom of this letter; nor could I come to the boldness of presenting it now, without another boldness, of putting his lordship, who now delivers it, to that office. Yet I have (or flatter myself to have) just excuses of this, and just ground of that ambition. For having obeyed at last, after much debatement within me, the inspirations (as I hope) of the Spirit of God, and resolved to make my profession Divinity, I make account, that I do but tell your Lordship what God hath told me, which is, that it is in their course, if in any, that my service may be of use to this Church and State. Since then your Lordship's virtues have made you so near the head in the one, and so religious a member of the other, I came to this courage of thrusting myself thus into your Lordship's presence, both in respect that I was an independent **and** disobliged man, towards any other person in this State: and delivered over now (in my resolution) to be a household servant of God. I humbly beseech your Lordship, that since these my purposes are likely to meet quickly a false and unprofitable dignity, which is the envy of others, you will vouchsafe to undertake, or prevent, or disable that, by affording them the true dignity of your just interpretations and favourable assistance. And to receive into your knowledge so much of the history and into your protection so much of the endeavours, of your Lordship's most humble and devoted servant.

'An independent and disobliged man' . . . it is a *cri de cœur*. Donne saw clearly that—in the words of Webster—'we are forced to woo because none dare woo us'. Five years had passed since he had turned down Morton's offer of a living (an offer made with the King's approval and encouragement), and now the initiative must come from himself. He had spent those five years in the constant study of theology, which he had enriched not only with poems (*La Corona*, the *Anniversaries*, and perhaps some of the holy sonnets), but also with a series of polemical works in which he had exorcised the ghosts of his Catholic forebears. In the former he reveals a deep religious faith, and in the latter an active intellectual preoccupation with religious differences and difficulties. If we want to try and fix the date of Donne's reconciliation to Anglicanism, or, at any rate, to chart the progress of that reconciliation, we may read his own clear and invaluable statement in the preface (addressed to the King) to one of his polemical works, *Pseudo-martyr*, published 1610:

They who have descended so low as to take knowledge of me and to admit me into their consideration, know well that I used no inordinate haste nor precipitation in binding

D

my conscience to any locall Religion. I had a longer worke to do than many other men; for I was first to blot out certaine impressions of the Romane religion, and to wrastle both against the examples and against the reasons, by which some hold was taken, and some anticipations early laid upon my conscience both by persons who by nature had a power and superiority over my will, and others who by their learning and good life seemed to me justly to claime an interest for the guiding and rectifying of mine understanding in these matters. And although I apprehended well enough, that this irresolution not only retarded my fortune but also bred some scandall and endangered my spiritual reputation, by laying me open to many misinterpretations, yet all these respects did not transport me to any violent and sudden determination till I had, to the measure of my poore wit and judgement, surveyed and digested the whole body of divinity, controverted between ours and the Romane church.

He wrote, too, at some time during his last years as a layman, his *Essays in Divinity*, not for publication but to clarify his own knowledge and work out his own position.

At the same time, he was fascinated by life and the world, and the State which was the microcosm of the universe, as much as he was fascinated by the 'little kingdom' of the human mind. It was inevitable that he should see that only a Church of England living could at one and the same time give him a recognized niche in the English political structure *and* satisfy his psychological drive towards religion. In the Church of England alone could a man place his theological learning at the service of the King and at the service of God. It was a political creation inseparable from the State and the Monarchy: a member of its hierarchy would be a minister of the Crown as well as a minister of God. It was the perfect solution to Donne's problem.

There could only have been one conceivable difficulty. Was he sure the Church of England was not a heresy? Was his conscience at last 'reconcileable to that rule'? Donne recorded his affirmative conclusion in the *Essays in Divinity*:

> . . . In my poor opinion, the form of God's worship established in the Church of England be more convenient and advantageous than of any other Kingdom, both to provoke and kindle devotion and also to fix it, that it stray not into infinite expansions and subdivisions, (into the former of which churches utterly despoiled of ceremonies seem to me to have fallen, and the Roman Church, by presenting innumerable objects, into the later). And though to all my thanksgivings to God I ever humbly acknowledge as one of his greatest mercies to me that he gave me my pasture in this park and my milk from the breasts of this church, yet out of a fervent and I hope not inordinate affection even to such a unity, I do zealously wish that the whole Catholic church were reduced to such unity and agreement in the form and profession established in any one of these Churches, (though ours were principally to be wished), which have not by any additions destroyed the foundation and possibility of Salvation in Christ Jesus.

It was a characteristically English conclusion. Yet it was no easy way out. Donne's religion never ceased to cause him doubts, reservations and, sometimes, a deep sense of error and despair. Like Dr. Johnson, he had read too much and thought too much for any calm, simple, childlike sense of security to be possible to him. He saw religion as a constant struggle, a constant rededication of a constantly unworthy soul, a constant modification in the face of life itself. The following notable and beautiful piece of self-revelation also comes from the *Essays in Divinity*. As usual, Donne puts his own position better than any apologist could:

. . . Hourly thou in thy Spirit descendest into my heart, to overthrow there legions of spirits of disobedience and incredulity and murmuring. . . . Thou hast set up many candlesticks and kindled many lamps in me, but I have either blown them out or carried them to guide me in bye or forbidden ways. Thou hast given me a desire of knowledge and some means to it, and some possession of it, and I have armed myself with Thy weapons against Thee. . . . But let me, in despite of me, be of so much use to thy Glory, that by thy mercy to my sin, other sinners may see how much sin thou canst pardon.

So the letter to Somerset was written. Somerset, however, was preoccupied with his own intricate private affairs. He needed lawyers, not clergymen, to procure for the Lady Frances Howard a divorce from the Earl of Essex in order that he might marry her himself. He got the divorce in the end, and there is no evidence that Donne was much help to him, but he might have thought that the ex-lawyer would be a useful man to have about. So he tried to persuade Donne to offer himself for a recently vacant clerkship of the council. It was an ironical proposition. Ten years ago, Donne would have jumped at it: even five years ago, he would probably have taken it. Now it was a whole world too late. The King himself intervened, and countered the suggestion of Somerset, whose influence was already declining, with a strong personal appeal to Donne to enter the ministry. 'I know Mr. Donne is a learned man and will prove a powerful preacher, and my desire is to prefer him that way, and in that way I will deny you nothing for him', the King told Somerset; and it seems feasible that the King's attitude and personal interest were as Walton records them. Donne himself, long afterwards, wrote of his 'old master's royal favours to me', and put as the chief of these the fact that James 'first inclined me to be a minister': and Walton continues with how 'after that time, the King descended to a persuasion, almost to a solicitation, of him to enter into sacred orders'. Donne did so early in 1615, in his forty-second year.

For Walton, as indeed for us, this was the central fact of Donne's life. 'Now', he writes triumphantly, 'the English Church had gained a second St. Austin.[1] . . . And now all his studies which had been occasionally diffused, were all concentred in Divinity. Now he had a new calling, new thoughts, and a new employment for his wit and eloquence: now all his earthly affections were changed into divine love.'

6. THE LAST YEARS

During the first year after his ordination, Donne continued to live in London. Under the system of that time, he was able to draw certain stipends from country benefices: others he refused because, as Walton says, 'he could not leave his beloved London'. He preached several times before the King at Whitehall, and in 1616 was elected Divinity Reader to the Benchers of Lincoln's Inn, a post involving the presentation of a weekly sermon to an extremely learned audience. It was a task for which both his scholastic and literary gifts fitted him perfectly.

In 1617 Donne's wife died. Only seven of her twelve children survived her. Her husband buried her in the church of St. Clement Danes, where her elaborate monument has long since perished. But the Latin epitaph he composed for her still survives, in a copy written in his own hand. 'To Ann daughter of George More of Loseley, a woman most choice, most beloved;

[1] i.e. Augustine.

a wife most dear, most pure; a mother most gentle, most dutiful; carried off by a cruel fever after fifteen years of marriage. Her husband, John Donne, made speechless by grief, sets up this stone to speak, pledges his ashes to hers in a new marriage under God. . . .' She was thirty-three. After her death, says Walton, Donne became 'crucified to the world'; and Donne himself testifies the same, in the beautiful Holy Sonnet (XVII) with which he commemorated her.

> Since she whom I lov'd hath payd her last debt
> To Nature, and to hers, and my good is dead,
> And her Soule early into heaven ravished,
> Wholly on heavenly things my mind is sett.

In May 1619 Donne made his last journey abroad. The King appointed him to accompany Viscount Doncaster's mission to arrange the Bohemian succession in favour of a Protestant ruler. Before leaving, he wrote the *Hymn to Christ, at the Author's last going into Germany*, the finest of his hymns. This poem can truly be described as both a prayer and a love-song. For Donne, with the death of his wife, all earthly loves are over, and he is not sorry; he asks Christ to

> Seale then this bill of my Divorce to All,
> On whom those fainter beames of love did fall;
> Marry those loves, which in youth scattered bee
> On Fame, Wit, Hopes (false mistresses) to thee.

As beautiful as the hymn is the sermon of farewell which he preached at Lincoln's Inn on 18 April 1619, a few weeks before he embarked. 'Remember me, not my abilities,' he asks, and his words echo the first verse of the *Hymn to Christ*: 'Christ Jesus remember us all in his Kingdom, to which, though we must sail through a sea, it is the sea of his blood, where no soul suffers shipwreck . . . where all clients shall retain but one counsellor, our Advocate Jesus Christ . . . where we shall be stronger to resist, and yet have no enemy; where we shall live and never die, where we shall meet and never part.'

'About a year after his return out of Germany,' says Izaak Walton,[1] 'the Deanry of St. Paul's being vacant, the King sent to Mr. Donne and appointed him to attend him at dinner the next day. When his Majesty was sat down, before he had eat any meat, he said after his pleasant manner, 'Dr. Donne, I have invited you to dinner; and though you sit not down with me, yet I will carve to you of a dish that I know you love well; for knowing you love London, I do therefore make you Dean of Paul's; and when I have dined, then do you take your beloved dish home to your study, say grace there to yourself, and much good may it do you.' This must have been some time in late August or early September 1621; Donne was installed on 27 November and remained Dean of St. Paul's until his death nearly ten years later: for he never attained—perhaps never wanted—a higher preferment. Perhaps, like Sydney Smith, he was too brilliant to be a safe choice as a bishop. In any case, he must have found in the deanery of St. Paul's an ideal home in which to pass his remaining years. He did much to beautify and restore the old church, and to improve the standard of the services. He preached the sermons at the great festivals of Easter, Whitsun and Christmas.

In October 1623 he became extremely ill of a fever from which he recovered slowly. In his sickness he began, and during a protracted convalescence completed, the remarkable prose work called the *Devotions*, 'in which', says Walton, 'the reader may see the most

[1] Hay's embassy returned to England in January 1620.

secret thoughts that then possessed his soul, paraphrased and made public'. Donne had often enough been a prey to disturbances of the mind, for which, as he himself had written, 'there is no criterium, no canon',[1] but now his mind was clear though his body was sick, and, as he saw death draw close and then recede, he was able to identify himself, through the Church which he served, with a sick and suffering humanity. Speaking to himself in a darkened room, he spoke to and for a larger congregation than even he would ever be able to preach to. 'My thoughts reach all, comprehend all.' Now, when he seemed most alone, most isolated, his mind soared to a supreme awareness of his oneness, through God, with mankind. He died into life, and saw in his ruin and recovery the rottenness and the redeemableness of man. The *Devotions* were published by Donne under his own name in 1624 and were reprinted four times in the next fifteen years.

At about the same time, he wrote his celebrated contribution to Anglican hymnology, the hymn *To God the Father* which he 'caused to be set to a most grave and solemn tune and to be often sung to the organ by the choristers of St. Paul's church in his own hearing' (Walton):[2]

> Wilt thou forgive that sinne where I begunne,
>   Which was my sin, though it were done before?
> Wilt thou forgive that sinne, through which I runne,
>   And do run still; though still I do deplore?
>   When thou hast done, thou hast not done,
>   For, I have more.

Donne's last years were spent in material comfort. In

[1] In a letter reprinted from the 1651 *Letters* by Gosse, *Life*, I, p. 184.
[2] A setting of the hymn by John Hilton is preserved in a mid-seventeenth-century MS. in the British Museum (Egerton MS. 2013, f. 13b), which *may* be the original tune referred to by Walton. Hilton was organist at St. Margaret's, Westminster, during the last few years of Donne's life.

addition to his stipend as Dean, he had the livings of Sevenoaks in Kent and Blunham in Bedfordshire, and in 1624 he was preferred to St. Dunstan's-in-the-West in the City of London. The following year, 1625, saw the death of James I. In that year the plague settled upon the capital, and in the autumn Donne took refuge in what was then the country village of Chelsea, in the house of his old friend Magdalen Herbert (now Lady Danvers). Two years later she too died, and Donne preached her funeral sermon with a heavy heart. 'She expected this that she hath received,' he said, feeling, perhaps, his own life 'ebbing out with them who homeward go'. But Walton records that he maintained his courage and cheerfulness, continued to preach his weekly sermon, and 'did prepare to leave the world before life left him'.

On 12 February 1631 he preached before King Charles for the last time. He had fallen ill while on a visit to his eldest daughter at Aldborough Hatch near Romford in Essex, but insisted upon making the wintry journey to London for his sermon. Walton's account of his delivery of that last sermon is as awe-inspiring as the sermon itself. His text was an uncompromising one: 'Unto God the Lord belong the issues from death' (Psalm 68, 20). 'And when,' writes Walton, 'to the amazement of some beholders he appeared in the Pulpit, many of them thought he presented himself not to preach mortification by a living voice, but mortality by a decayed body and a dying face. . . . Many that then saw his tears, and heard his faint and hollow voice, professing they thought the text prophetically chosen, and that Dr. Donne had preached his own funerall sermon.' The man that Walton and the rest of the congregation saw in the pulpit that bleak February day in Whitehall was almost, already, the statue he would soon become. Donne's

Jacobean sense of drama did not fail him now as he spoke for the last time:

> We have a winding sheet in our mothers' wombe, which grows with us from our conception, and wee come into the world, wound up in that winding sheet; for we come to seek a grave. . . . This whole world is but an universall churchyard, but our common grave. . . . That which we call life is but *Hebdomada mortium*, a week of deaths, seven days, seven periods of our life spent in dying, a dying seven times over, and there is an end.

Donne was himself among the last of the great Jacobeans. Within a few years of his death, which occurred on the last day of March 1631, those few of his contemporaries who had outlived him died also; George Herbert in 1633, Chapman and Marston in 1634, Ben Jonson in 1637. It was the end of an era, and Donne's last sermon is its fitting epitaph. 'Our youth is worse thar our infancy, and our age worse than our youth.' In Donne, pessimism had been sometimes a fashion, but it had the last word, a peculiarly Jacobean last word. Fantastic? Yes, the funeral sermon may seem so. But as Donne himself wrote, long before, 'to be fantastick in young men is conceitfull distemperature, and a witty madness; but in old men whose senses are withered it becomes natural, therefore more full and perfect. For as when we sleep our fancy is most strong, so it is in age which is a slumber of the deep sleep of death.'

PART II

THE METAPHYSICAL SCHOOL

D ONNE, like other sixteenth-century poets—e.g.
Wyatt, Ralegh and Sidney—did not allow his poems
to fall into the printer's hands. Many people must have
possessed manuscript copies[1] of Donne's elegies, satires,
hymns, sonnets and love-poems, but it was not until
1633 that the poems were first printed. Their influence
and stature grew, so that in the 1640's the man whom
Ben Jonson had called 'the first poet in the world in
some things' became the dead leader of a very live
'school' of poets, which has been known since the
eighteenth century (when the whole school was attacked
by Samuel Johnson) as the metaphysical school. Its
chief poets are Donne, Herbert, King, Vaughan, Carew,
Cowley, Crashaw, Marvell and (in his early poems only)
Milton. An excellent representative selection of the
poems of these and other poets of the school was edited
by Sir Herbert Grierson in 1921. That anthology drew
from T. S. Eliot his celebrated essay in rehabilitation,
from which our modern recognition of Donne as a
major poet may be said to date.

Johnson's term 'metaphysical' has caused some confusion. Though he includes some quotations from
Donne, he is writing primarily about Cowley, who was
born nearly fifty years after Donne and who sometimes
used images in Donne's learned manner, but who wrote

---

[1] A considerable number of these survives, many dating from the second
quarter of the seventeenth century, when Donne was most fashionable.

a different and lesser kind of poetry. Nor does Johnson mean by 'metaphysical' that Donne and Cowley were philosophical poets like Dante and Lucretius. Donne does not use poetry to set forth metaphysics, but uses his knowledge of Plato, Aristotle, the medieval philosophers and the new learning, when he writes his poetry. The label 'metaphysical' is a literary label.

Johnson's attack on the school is an attack on their misplaced learning ('to show their learning was their whole endeavour'), though he also observes that 'to write like them it is at least necessary to read and think'. He also attacked their use of imagery ('they broke every image into fragments'), and, along with this, their concept, as he saw it, of 'wit-writing': 'A combination of dissimilar images, or discovery of occult resemblances in things apparently unlike.' Much of this, of course, is true, particularly of Donne's imitators. (But with the passage of time practices that to Johnson were faults have become regarded as virtues.) Johnson also realized the importance of wit[1] in the metaphysicals but although he is writing about Cowley, he misses Cowley's own excellent definition of wit:

> In a true piece of Wit all things must be,
>   Yet all things there agree;
> As in the **Ar**k,[2] joined without force or strife,
> All creatures dwelt, all creatures that had life,
>   Or as the primitive force of all
>   (If we compare great things with small)
>   Which, without discord or confusion, lie
>   In that strange mirror of the Deity.

Today, we should rather define wit along Cowley's own lines, as an all-embracing quality of the free,

---

[1] See T. S. Eliot's essay on Andrew Marvell.

[2] Perhaps Cowley remembered Donne's line about wisdom making man 'an Arke where all agree' (*Letter to Sir Edw. Herbert*, 2).

original, creative mind. At its best, in, say, Marvell's *To His Coy Mistress*, it is Coleridge's Imagination, 'essentially vital', welding by passion all things into one: it is the reconciling of what were thought to be opposites. At a lower level, it is Coleridge's Fancy, 'playing with fixities and definitions', the slave of an arbitrary and often absurd choice. Some of the more tedious and tasteless metaphysical conceits are witty in this lower, arbitrary sense.

But however all-embracing we make our definition of wit as a quality of the cultivated European mind, involving more than mere felicity, more even than urbanity, sophistication or tough irony, we shall still be speaking of a quality not peculiar to Donne. What makes his poems unique, and unclassifiable in a way that Cowley's are not unclassifiable, is simply his greatness as a poet of the English language, a creator of his own modes. Johnson puts him with Cowley among the 'metaphysicals': but he towers above Cowley, and above all his contemporaries save Shakespeare. His poems are a peculiar blend of medieval learning (interest in ideas) and Renaissance *esprit* (interest in human behaviour). His philosophic ideas are largely traditional (platonic, scholastic, jesuit), but the attitudes to, the analyses and the expression of these ideas in language, uniquely differentiate his poems. In them, the old and the new are held in tense conflict. The poems express his personality; they are the living voice of English literature, like the poetry of Shakespeare.

Donne's literary technique is often dramatic and rhetorical. His arresting opening lines like 'For Godsake hold your tongue, and let me love' are meant to capture the reader's attention. Once the attention is captured dramatically, it can then be exploited by analysing a situation verbally as an idea. A poem of Donne is often an argument in which a mind trained in analogy, in seeing one thing in terms of others (the essential training of logic and metaphysics), exploits a chosen situation with a new and elaborate set of interconnected images. Donne enormously and significantly widened the range of private verse (lyric, satire, elegy, meditation). His best poems are voyages of discovery as important as any made by his contemporaries in geography and adventure: voyages of the mind which

> creates, transcending these,
> Far other worlds and other seas.

Inheriting from his contemporaries and immediate predecessors the immense yet formal Elizabethan world-picture, a true son of the Renaissance, Donne came to maturity in the age of disenchantment that followed the Golden Age. His own decade of anxiety, 1601–10, mirrored that of the age, and rendered him peculiarly sensitive to the dark side of the human condition.

> Study me then, you who shall lovers bee
> At the next world, that is, at the next Spring:
>> For I am every dead thing,
>> In whom love wrought new Alchimie.

In this way he could set his own personal reactions within the framework of the age which he studied, and to which he responded so accurately. Thus his poems often seem curiously alive and up-to-date, for they are the secret writings of an introspective intellectual, with no position in the society in which he suffered and learned, making articulate the private rebellions and difficulties which underlay his restless and dissatisfied generation. In a different way, a number of T. S. Eliot's early poems do the same thing: hence his emphasis on Donne and the revival of interest in an author thought unsuitable by Palgrave for inclusion in the *Golden Treasury*. In the recent past he has perhaps even been overpraised. Nevertheless, the ultimate tribute due to him, and we cannot fail to pay it, is that he must be judged by the highest possible criteria. When he died, Thomas Browne, Henry King, Carew, Walton and others of the younger generation (the generation to which he will always appeal most) paid him their tribute of funeral elegies, written largely in the manner that he himself had invented. By his death the 'universal monarchy of wit' had been left, not without its courtiers, but without a king.

PART III

SECULAR POEMS

I. SONGS AND SONETS[1]

THESE are the fifty-five secular lyrics, in various metres and written at various times (the majority before he took orders), on which Donne's reputation as an original love-poet principally rests. The collection was first published by the poet's son in 1633. But during Donne's lifetime many of the poems circulated in manuscript in the small London literary world and were highly prized by those lucky enough to get hold of copies. Constantine Huyghens, the Dutch poet and scholar, who seems to have become acquainted with Donne about 1618, wrote in 1630 to his friend and fellow-poet Hooft: 'In poetry Donne is more famous than anyone. Many rich fruits from the green branches of his wit have lain mellowing among the lovers of art, which now, when nearly rotten with age, they are distributing. Into my hands have fallen . . . some 25 of the best sort.' Huyghens does not say what the poems were, but from their number alone it is certain that some 'songs and sonets' must have been included: and we know that he translated some of them into Dutch. Huyghens's letter shows that by 1630 Donne's position as a dignitary of the Church and his great reputation as a

---

[1] 'Sonet' is connected with 'sonata', and was used of any short poem in song form such as might be (though need not be) set to music. There are no *sonnets* in the collection.

preacher had reawakened interest in the brilliant compositions of his youth which he had never officially offered to the world. In Donne's own time, poetic taste would certainly have regarded his early satires and elegies as the revolutionary equals of *Songs and Sonets*: but today it is probably the latter which are the most widely read of all his poems.

I have been able to discover only one poem in the collection which found its way into print while Donne was still alive: this is *Breake of Daye*, an *aubade* in the popular manner, which almost alone of the collection bears small trace of Donne's peculiar characteristics, and might have been written by anybody. It appears, in full, though unattributed, in a small collection of songs with music, William Corkine's *Second Booke of Ayres*, published in 1612, three years before Donne took orders. It may well have been written not long before that date and have attracted Corkine's attention as suitable material for his anthology.

A few of the *Songs and Sonets*, such as *A Valediction: forbidding mourning*, have been linked to actual events and people in Donne's life, but the majority need only to be thought of as expressions of moments of intense emotional activity inside the poet's mind—that is, their only correspondence to reality is to inner reality, not to any biographically identifiable facts. Although the poems are love-poems, it is not necessary to search for the source of their inspiration in actual people. Some, by their tenderness and unwonted gentleness, may be helpfully associated with one specific woman, the poet's wife; the tone of one or two others may suggest them to have been addressed to Lucy Countess of Bedford as elaborate half-serious 'test-pieces': but of the majority it is enough to say that they are literary experiments, explorations of the love-relationship from,

of course, the man's point of view. They should be read
as poems, each complete in itself as a real object capable
of being admired and studied alone on the page: not as
clues to biography. No poem of any merit can be made
to depend on anything but itself.

The order of the poems in the published editions is
not chronological: and many of them are unlikely ever
to be certainly dated. Not all of them belong to the
fifteen-nineties, though the majority probably do. Some
of them indeed can confidently be dated after 1598—
several of these because they seem to be related to the
period of Donne's courtship and marriage. Others are
possibly, from their darker mood and more profound
harmonies, even later: one at least seems to have been
inspired by sorrow at the death of his wife. Metrically,
the poems exhibit great variety and originality: nearly
all of them are in different metres, mostly stanza forms
of Donne's own invention repeated neither by himself
nor by any later poet. But although the individual metres
are many, they all share the same quality of metric,
produce the same kinds of metrical effect, and spring
from the same attitude to metre. This quality, this
effect, this attitude, are not paralleled in the works of
any earlier poet. Coleridge pointed out that in poems
where the author thinks, and expects the reader to do
so, the sense must be understood in order to ascertain
the metre. And it was Coleridge who said that 'to
read Dryden, Pope, etc., you need only count syllables; but to read Donne you must measure Time,
and discover the time of each word by the sense of
Passion'.

You cannot separate the metre from the other components of a Donne poem: the metre is part of the fused
whole, not something 'superadded'. The very pauses
are like the pauses between phrases in music: they are

as important as the phrases themselves. Donne must be read with an ear to his silences as well as his words, and with an appreciation of his power to syncopate. A good way to grasp the movement, as well as the sense, of one of the stanzas in *Songs and Sonets* is to read it aloud:

> When my grave is broke up againe
> Some second ghest to entertaine,
> (For graves have learn'd that woman-head
> To be to more then one a Bed)
> And he that digs it, spies
> A bracelet of bright haire about the bone,
> Will he not let'us alone,
> And thinke that there a loving couple lies,
> Who thought that this device might be some way
> To make their soules, at the last busie day,
> Meet at this grave, and make a little stay?
>
> *The Relique*, Stanza 1.

This poem contains three stanzas, each having eleven lines, of which the first four are octosyllabic or four-footed lines, the fifth and seventh six-syllabled or three-footed, and the remainder of the length and pattern of the blank verse line (decasyllabic). In reading this stanza aloud, one sees that the first two lines, regular and equal, broach the theme with a typical Donnian startlingness and boldness: lines 3 and 4 have the same length as 1 and 2, but their being enclosed in brackets, and the dig at woman's inconstancy which they offer (the meaning is, graves have learnt the feminine trick of being a bed to more than one person: old graves were often dug up to make room for new tenants),[1] show that they should be read and thought of with less intensity than line 2, with, if read aloud, a lowering and quickening of the voice; the closing of the bracket serves

[1] 'that' in line 3 is of course the adjective and must be fully sounded.

for a tiny pause before line 5 is read: but that line is shorter than lines 1–4 by a foot (two syllables), and returns, with still greater concreteness and strength, to the situation as it was left after line 2, before that mocking little parenthesis slipped in: so we can afford to pause after line 4 in part compensation for the brevity and in preparation for the major *recoup* of line 5. This line's shortness is, as it were, disguised by the two powerful monosyllabic verbs, and there is of course no pause before line 6 which is an obvious emotional climax: it is the first 'full length' line, and moreover reaches the maximum length attained anywhere in the stanza. The poetical beauty of the alliteration of 'b', the sense of continuing life in the phrase 'bright haire', associated here with something dead (bone), combine to create a very powerful emotional effect on the reader: and we cannot but pause here, taking into account the shortness of the next line, for slightly longer than we should if line 7 were as long as line 6 or even as long as line 4. Line 7 hurries us on, dismissing the wonder of the gravedigger's discovery. The apostrophe between 'let' and 'us' signifies a syncopation: the two syllables must have only the time of one.[1] Then we can broaden out, for the rest of the stanza, in a justification of line 7. The 'commentary' in lines 8–11 will probably take nearly as long to read as the 'exclamation', the 'presentation', of 1–7.

The poem, which is one of Donne's most celebrated and characteristic, must now be considered as a whole.

---

[1] Elision is frequent in Donne, and provides variation from the basic or normal line in a stanza pattern, e.g.:

Beaut(y) a convenient type may be to figure it
(Alexandrine: *A Valediction : of the Booke*).
My love was infinite if spring make (i)t more
(Blank verse line: *Love's Growth*).
His onl(y) and onl(y) his purse
(Six-syllabled line: *The Curse*).

If this fall in a time, or land,
Where mis-devotion doth command,
Then, he that digges us up, will bring
Us, to the Bishop, and the King,
    To make us reliques; then
Thou shalt be a Mary Magdalen, and I
    A something else thereby;
All women shall adore us, and some men;
And since at such time, miracles are sought,
I would have that age by this paper taught
What miracles wee harmlesse lovers wrought.

First, we lov'd well and faithfully,
Yet knew not what wee lov'd, nor why,
Difference of sex no more wee knew,
    Then our Guardian Angells doe;
        Comming and going, wee
Perchance might kisse, but not between those meales;
    Our hands ne'r toucht the seales,
Which nature, injur'd by late law, sets free:
These miracles wee did: but now alas,
All measure, and all language, I should passe,
Should I tell what a miracle shee was.

Some critics of Donne have tried to establish exactly
what woman in his life called forth this sort of poem
and have tried to associate the different tones and attitudes of various lyrics with different women. But when
Donne was criticized for his hyperbolic praise of
Elizabeth Drury in his *Anniversaries*, he replied that 'he
described the idea of a woman and not as she was'. That
is a clue we ought to use in reading other poems as well
as the *Anniversaries*. Naturally, it is important—and
impossible—not to miss a difference of intention between poems like the *Song* 'Sweetest love, I do not
goe', or the *Valediction: forbidding mourning*, which by
their spirituality and absence of irony are clearly different
in tone and attitude, in which an actual and very simple

emotional situation is presented to Donne and accepted with as much simplicity as was ever possible to him—between these, and poems like *The Relique*, which by its fanciful nature and its indulgence in witty hyperbole, is an example of a situation realized as a logical conceit and offered as an artifice. Not in *The Relique*, then, nor in the majority of the *Songs and Sonets*, does Donne

> Put to proof art alien to the artist's,
> Once, and only once, and for one only,
> So to be the man and leave the artist,
> Gain the man's joy, miss the artist's sorrow.

These lines seem to illuminate this whole problem of the 'sincerity' and 'seriousness' of Donne's love-poems. They are from Browning's 'One Word More', in which, as an epilogue to *Men and Women*, he asks his wife to

> Let me speak this once in my true person.

And what is the poet's 'true person'? For his wife, a man the world need never know. For the world—well, 'the rest are all men's', so that we do not need to worry too much lest we may be taking a poem of Donne too seriously, or not seriously enough, provided that we take it as a *poem*, and not as an entry in a diary.

The Relique is characteristic of Donne's peculiar wit, which, in a perfectly untechnical sense, we might call fancy. There is always a sense of the whole situation being *held back* even while it is presented. The grave of the poet, dug up in time hence, reveals him wearing round his arm a lock of a woman's hair. Let the disturber of death, says Donne, fancy that this was our device to stay together—as we were in life—without bodily togetherness. Then it might happen (continues the poet), in an unchristian or wrongly Christian land, that I am adored as a 'relic'—the 'something else' is presumably Christ: in that case, we ought to provide some miracles in advance. But we have done that: we have provided the miracle of a platonic love affair, to conduct which a woman must herself be something of a miracle.

Such a fancy makes no sense outside the realm of poetry, where it was created, i.e. outside this poem. It is, empirically, meaningless: its propositions remain untestable hypotheses; but it has produced a brilliant and curiously moving poem; for although the tone and suggestions are light—the poet willingly and constantly puts himself in another's place and regards himself with amused detachment—yet the basic situation of the despoiled grave, and the passion of that sixth line, 'A bracelet of bright haire about the bone', ringing down through the rest of the piece, supply the necessary underlying reality in terms which, wherever they occur, cannot be taken wholly 'unseriously'.

The poem is a new kind of love-poem. There is the love of the dead poet as it is actually supposed to have been, described in the last stanza; there is the device, introduced at the beginning of the poem, by which the poet fancies himself, before death, to have symbolized his love-story even in the grave; and, in between, there is the (absurd) result fancied as possibly arising from so (absurd) a love-affair:

> All women shall adore us, and some men.

This line, neatly hitting off a sexual difference of attitude both to religion and to love (i.e. women taking both forms of adoration, on the whole, more seriously than men), is central to the poem. Donne slyly points out that he doesn't suppose his 'fancy' will take in his own sex, the fanciful sex, wholesale, as it will woman, the literal sex. The poem imagines true love commemorated at death in a symbol (the bracelet) of passionate, but

purely private and profane, emotional significance—
'will he not let us alone?' Then is introduced the dig
at (chiefly) feminine literalness and gullibility—if the
dead lovers are *not* left alone, it will be because the
bracelet has given someone the absurd idea that they are
relics of religious power. Yet this fantastic possibility
can be justified, and is so in the poem, by means of that
central image of the bracelet, which, with the line 'all
women shall adore us and some men', is the key to the
poem's meaning. The bracelet, meant to equal 'true
love', will be thought to equal 'miracle'. But true love
is a miracle: the play on 'miracle' produces subtly inter-
locking ideas of profane and sacred love which the
fantastic poet can reconcile even as he demonstrates how
the literal and gullible will confuse them.

Thus the metaphysical and ideal conceit, when employed by an artist of major sensibility, can produce a
poem which is fantastic without affectation, witty
without triviality and original without absurdity. *The
Relique* can give satisfaction as a work of art although it
treats the traditional theme of love in an unconventional
manner. It is a less 'serious' poem than, say, *The
Extasie*, because it treats love less intensely, less uni-
versally, and says less about man, the ultimate subject
of all verse. Its tone needs to be judged with peculiar
nicety, blending as it does passion, romance and the
ironic in an urbane, civilized but slightly *outré* manner
which places it immediately as the product of that
unique English phenomenon, the cultivated Jacobean
mind.

A metaphysical poem seeks to build up a sense of
intellectual and intelligible order out of a number of
disparate images. The images are apparently unrelated
and, it has been argued by Johnson and others, unrelat-
able. But, for the metaphysical poet, they have got

nevertheless to be related. When they are, the result is a metaphysical poem. The basis of such a poem is not musical and decorative, but intellectual and ideal: ideal in the sense of that word's connection with *idea*: ideal as opposed to 'real'. 'I described the idea of a woman, not as she was': and Plato's philosophy presupposes behind every actual thing in the world an 'idea', present to the mind of the first creator, an abstract concept to the pattern of which all concrete examples are made. Behind every observation about love is the concept of love itself. This may seem to contradict the psychological realism so characteristic of Donne,

> For Godsake hold your tongue, and let me love,

but this is not so. Donne uses the real: but it is the ideal, in the sense of the idea, that lies in brightness behind the tangible shadows he describes: the idea as that to which all concrete offspring or exemplars must, to make sense, be ultimately and implicitly related. Donne has a poem in *Songs and Sonets* about a flea; what could be more 'real'? An early Elizabethan would not have written a lyric about a flea, for his aim was, in a lyric or song, to idealize the real, to decorate it with appropriate verbal beauties, with which such a subject would have been incompatible. But Donne's aim is to realize the ideal: and as Plato said, the ideal can only be approached through the 'real' which is in fact its shadow; the world of touch, taste, sight and sense, apparently so vivid, is only a phenomenon that dies with us, a reflection in our world of the eternal, timeless, absolute values and realities in heaven, which he called 'ideas' or forms. It is in that sense that Cowley, in his famous definition of wit, spoke of 'primitive forms', the prime absolute ideas of God. What has this to do with a flea? This: Donne's flea does not remain a flea for long: it has bitten and sucked the blood of both the poet and his mistress

> This flea is you and I, and this
> Our mariage bed, and mariage temple is. . . .

It is not merely decorated with verbal felicities: wit has translated it. The flea is seen as one of the million created objects of this life, all equal because they all add up to the created world, and all capable of being related to seemingly disparate because, to our taste, 'higher' things, if one posits the unifying concept of a creator who made the universe as an order full of hidden relationships which the poet, creator of his own little world of a poem, can in that poem discover, arrange and reveal. There is in fact something of a paradox to be faced here. Donne is intensely 'modern' in his psychological realism: but behind his vivid presentation of our material world, organizing it and enabling him to choose what he wants and connect as he wants, is his Renaissance belief in ideas as the true reality of a thinking man, the only begetters of those earthly shadows which we taste, and touch, and go to bed with, and which die. It is that which makes his realism possible and gives it its power not merely to startle and convince, but to thrill and move us.

In another poem, *A Valediction: of weeping*,[1] Donne conjures up a relationship a good deal more ironical and Petrarchan than anything in the simpler *Valediction: forbidding mourning* written possibly for his wife (although the compass image in the last three verses of that piece is a sufficiently curious conceit to have stirred Dr. Johnson's indignation). Its theme is the parting of a man from a woman, at which the man weeps 'and knows why'. His tears, as they fall before her face, are called coins: they bear her stamp both

[1] See W. Empson, *Seven Types of Ambiguity*, pp. 175-83, for an illuminating discussion of this poem.

because they can reflect her image (the tear as a mirror: Donne's verse is full of mirrors and reflections—in *Witchcraft by a Picture* the poet's eye is reflected in the woman's), and because she has called them forth, made them, signed them and hence given them value: he is weeping because of her, which is why his tears are 'fruits of much griefe'. They are also 'emblemes of more' because

> When a teare falls, that thou falst which it bore.

His tear, signed by her image, falls to the ground: her reflection in it falls also. But 'thou falst' surely also means 'falst from grace', 'art unfaithful': as her image falls, so she will; and the thought of this is cause and signal for him to weep afresh:

> So thou and I are nothing then, when on a divers shore.

'So' means 'so that I perceive that': just as his tear falls, and her image with it, into nothing, so her love, as soon as they are apart, is nothing too. The whole verse, with its tear imagery, is undeniably sad, and at first reading unaccountably so. But when we see the underlying point of her unfaithfulness (nowhere is the word used or the accusation made directly), the culminating tear-images and the slow-moving gentle sorrow of the verse gain in power and significance.

In verse two, the tear is compared to a globe which is blank (nothing) until the cartographer has painted on it a copy of the world: then it is 'All'. So his tears with her image (a copy of her) reflected in them change from meaningless drops into worlds

> Till thy teares mixt with mine doe overflow
> This world, by waters sent from thee, my heaven dissolved so.

She is his heaven: her tears are rain which, commingling

with the world of his own tears, dissolves that world. This verse is highly ingenious and very difficult: the poet's tears stand for the world, made out of nothings (empty globes of water) by her image, while *her* tears, achieving only the ironically-meant *physical* comparison to a flood, promptly drown that world when she, too, weeps. This leads us directly to the impassioned apostrophe of the woman

> O more then Moone,
> Draw not up seas to drowne me in thy spheare,

in which he begs her not to weep, for her tears are destructive. All through the poem, this point has been built up, and fresh proof of the sinister meaning of 'When a teare falls, that thou falst which it bore' is now offered. Her tears are destructive because false: they can do him no good and she had much better, therefore, not weep at all, but leave that to him. And, in final reproach, the poet adds: 'Do not sigh. If I go overseas, waves and wind may kill me anyhow. Your destructive sighs and tears can only add to my distress.' He forbids her to express emotions which he feels are as false and destructive as the elements.

The amount of irony in this poem is the amount required to enable the reader to swallow it. It is clear that the poem's ingenuity is extraordinary. Yet without a grasp of the workings of that ingenuity we are not prepared to understand the undoubtedly fine emotional climax at the beginning of the last stanza. Donne is here attempting the following argument: 'I am sad because I am leaving you to go abroad. I weep because I fear that separation will end our love. You are weeping now, I see, more copiously than I, but your tears are merely physical (merely woman's) and destructive of love: while mine are "real" (i.e. intellectual) things, worlds containing all of you. Do not, therefore, weep, because by so doing you annihilate my valuable tears with your valueless ones which, being valueless, kill me because they show me you do not really care. And if your tears are like rain, or the sea, your sighs (for now you sigh) are like the wind. Do not anticipate now what the real elements may well achieve when I go abroad.'

To revert for a moment to the *Song* 'Sweetest love, I do not goe', the fourth verse of that piece organizes similar material in a completely different way and with entirely different implications:

> When thou sigh'st, thou sigh'st not winde,
>   But sigh'st my soule away,
> When thou weep'st, unkindly kinde,
>   My lifes blood doth decay.
>   It cannot bee
> That thou lov'st mee, as thou say'st,
> If in thine my life thou waste,
>   Thou art the best of mee.

This poem was written by Donne on the occasion of his leaving for Germany when his wife was pregnant and worried. It is not a perfectly pellucid poem, but in comparison with *A Valediction: of weeping* it is simple and old-fashioned in its form and manner. It does not seem fanciful to suppose that it was written and given to Ann for her to read and keep and console herself with while he was away. Even if this biographical allusion is questioned, the poem may still be felt as sharing with *A Valediction forbidding mourning* an almost stoical tone and a deliberate rejection of the stock Petrarchan treatment of the theme of absence: here seen not as cause for complaint and despair, but as something natural and inevitable. In both these poems experience is shared, not dramatised as the peculiar prerogative of the poet-lover; and simultaneously spiritualised (by proclaiming an ideal love which survives separation) and played down (by being reduced to the oddly comforting form of an Elizabethan song). In the reassuring pattern (as in the simple traditional quatrains of the *Valediction*) absence itself is made unimportant by abandoning rhetoric.

In the poem *Of weeping*, the subject is the intellectual significance and point of the man's feelings as they struggle to render themselves articulate against the 'natural', spontaneous but wholly empty protestations (physical sighs and tears) of the woman. Both poet and woman appear to react identically to the situation: but the psychological difference is made clear by the poet's use of a single common symbol-object, a tear. The implied assessment of the feminine role in heterosexual love occurs frequently throughout *Songs and Sonets*. Sometimes it is less subtle and sad, more brutal and cynical, e.g. in *The Indifferent*:

> I can love any, so she be not true

or in *Communitie* with its notorious, rakish ending:

> And when hee hath the kernell eate,
> Who doth not fling away the shell?

Sometimes, as in *Of weeping*, it is the intellectual who is speaking, and beneath the jesting irony lies the psychological statement which saves Donne's best metaphysical poems from being *merely* conceit and nothing else, e.g. in *Loves Alchymie*, which ends

> Hope not for minde in women; at their best
> Sweetnesse and wit, they'are but *Mummy*, possest.

Loves Deitie illustrates well the realism with which Donne can write about the idea of the love-relationship. The celebrated opening

> I long to talke with some old lovers ghost,
> Who dyed before the god of Love was borne

propounds the warning that 'love' has many meanings, and that the modern torment of Petrarchan love is very different from the love of the lovers of old; by 'the god of love' Donne clearly means all the *angst* available in his time to the psychologically-instructed intellectual who is so unwise as to submit to the human bondage of loving 'her who loves not me'. Before 'love' was deified, i.e. made a cult, it was simple and true. The original 'office' or function of Cupid was

> indulgently to fit
> Actives to passives. Correspondencie
> Only his subject was;

Donne recognizes, even in 'true love', the abiding platonic principle that one will call and one answer, one pursue and the other be pursued. But nevertheless, in the 'golden age', Cupid stepped in only 'when an even flame two hearts did touch', and the conclusion to this (the second) stanza is firm:

> It cannot bee
> Love, till I love her, that loves mee.

But nowadays, all the modern talk about 'love' means something far more complex. It is no longer a simple matter of 'correspondencie'. Love for a young intellectual (the poem is almost certainly an early one, written in the fifteen-nineties) has become a thraldom to the sort of wretched passion described by Somerset Maugham in *Of Human Bondage*. If only we could wake up, could see that 'romantic' love meant nothing but misery, we could get rid of all its nonsensical apparatus of 'rage, lust, letter writing, commendations', and free ourselves from affairs with those who care nothing for us.

But in the last stanza, we feel the sting in the tail. 'My complaints are unwise: this isn't the worst love can do to a man. It might turn me against loving altogether: that is, it might prevent the possibility of a future genuine relationship: the game must go on, for the sake of a possible victory one day; or, worst of all, *she* might suddenly feel the same way about me as I do now about her. If she did, this would only add lies to indifference: I know she has loved someone before, and if she should fall for me it would prove her earlier declarations false and, *a fortiori*, her new ones to me could scarcely be relied on either. So one is in a cleft stick, and must endure one's *angst*.' In this last stanza, with its analysis of the meanings of 'love', Donne states a possibility in such a way as to dispense with any whole-hearted immersion of one's feelings in the finality of that possibility. He can write about love with detachment as effectively as he can write about it with emotion: but the emotion is rarely quite naïve, and when it is, as in 'Sweetest love, I do not goe', we may feel that Petrarchan sophistication is being rejected in favour of something to which the poet is more deeply committed and (therefore) vulnerable: while in *Loves Deitie* he seeks invulnerability from the god of love by constructing a logical, ironic defence against him.

In *The Legacie* we return to the method of analysing the love-relationship by a 'metaphysical' deploying of a single word-object which belongs to such relationships. In *A Valediction: of weeping* it was tears; in this poem it is a heart. The title, and much of the poem's imagery, depend on the familiar notion that absence from the loved one is death. Before he left her last time ('When I dyed last') the poet is sure he promised her, by way of a legacy, some gift. If he were really dead, he could not remember, so a split-personality trick is introduced whereby the essential fake involved in the 'absence= death' equation is both admitted and ignored at the same time, so that Donne can write

F

> Though I be dead, which sent mee, I should be
> Mine own executor and Legacie.

He has 'survived himself' into a kind of death-in-life of
separation, where

> I heard mee say, Tell her anon,
> That my selfe, (that is you, not I)
> Did kill me. . . .

(she was all of his real self, so that by leaving him alone
she was responsible for his death), and where he recalls
that

> I bid mee send my heart, when I was gone,

But he could not find his heart, and was forced to lie to
her by leaving what he did not have: the implication is
that she already had his heart, whole and entire and completely in her possession. The imagery of death is sustained, and the brilliant, violent line in which he describes
(still the dual personality) Donne A (alive) searching
Donne B (a corpse) for his heart, is worth quoting:

> When I had ripp'd me,' and search'd where hearts did lye;

In the last verse, there is a remarkable change of tone, a
deepening, a refocusing, which is technically and spiritu-
ally magnificent. The schism is healed, there is no more
Donne A and Donne B; the ironically macabre 'situation'
created in the first two verses has made its point, and can
now fade gradually into the final reproach, the last
accusation:

> Yet I found something like a heart,
> But colours it, and corners had,
> It was not good, it was not bad,
> It was intire to none, and few had part.
> As good as could be made by art
> It seem'd; and therefore for our losses sad,

> I meant to send this heart instead of mine,
> But oh, no man could hold it, for twas thine.

This verse is vibrant with a still ironic regret, yet in no sense, in spite of the conceit of the foregoing stanzas which it develops, can it not be called 'serious'. Her heart is given wholly to no man, and what he found was a part of it only: that small part which he *did* play in her life.

This and the previous poem might be described as an ironic Petrarchan exercise, far from the pastoral sentimentality of:

> My true love hath my heart and I have his
> By just exchange one for the other given.

Sidney's sweet sonnet belongs indeed to the days 'before the god of Love was borne': here is very 'corresponden-cie'. But in *The Legacie* Donne again contrasts a man's silly romanticism with a woman's practical promiscuity. The latter can so divide her heart that she keeps it still, yet many men are tormented by the fear of only possessing a scrap (a 'corner') of her affection which sticks inside them and makes them (unless they are perceptive enough to see and face the truth) dream they possess what they can never possess. The emotional effect of that slow, regular closing couplet is important, because it warns us against being led, by the trick-imagery of this very Renaissance piece of rhetorical poetry, into dismissing what is being said as 'unreal' or 'insincere'.

Certain lighter pieces in *Songs and Sonets* are, indeed, little more than *jeux d'esprit*. Among these are *The Paradox*, a neat rhetorical demonstration that loving is like dying and hence, if genuinely experienced, impossible to describe; the *Song*, 'Goe, and catche a falling starre'[1]

---

[1] There is a musical setting of this piece in a seventeenth-century MS. in the British Museum, Egerton MS. 2013.

on the impossibility of finding a faithful woman; and *Womans Constancy* (the title is a sardonic hit, the theme being her inconstancy). But even in such conventional exercises, the work of Donne's bachelor days, we find significant moments of psychological perception of the relativeness of time and of guessable truth: she may be true now, but in a moment she will be false and

> say that now
> We are not just those persons, which we were.

In the dark, uncertain days before he found anchorage in the emblem of Christ, Donne was naturally a creature of moods and circumstance, and in moments of exasperation, disappointment and disillusion must often have apostrophized himself with the lines with which his fifth *Satire* ends:

> Thou'art the swimming dog whom shadows cosened,
> And div'st, near drowning, for what's vanished.

The wonder is, considering those shadows, that cynicism, in its modern sense, is so rarely a dominant mood in Donne's verse. Good humour, a clear wit and a very Jacobean sense of the tragicomedy of life, so often have the last word: and even *Womans Constancy* ends with Donne abstaining from arguing with a woman who has her excuses for fickleness ready upon her tongue, because (how urbane the admission is)

> by to morrow, I may thinke so too.

   ·   ·   ·   ·   ·   ·   ·   ·

One of the most famous of Donne's poems in *Songs and Sonets* is *The Extasie*. In this poem, an essential philosophy is put forward with remarkably little ironic reserve. Here, apparently, the word 'sex' is used in its modern sense for the first time. The Platonic 'ladder' of sex, leading from the actual physical relationship to the 'idea' of love as it is in heaven, leads Donne to Plato's immortality, and to the idea of a rebirth and new knowledge of the personality achieved by the fusion of the two lovers' souls. 'Ecstasy' is a technical term of the Christian mystics for a state of extreme and abnormal awareness: it means, literally, a 'standing outside', which is just what happens here. The souls leave their bodies and stand outside them, raised to a new power as a single observer-soul, able to reveal the truth about love.

> This Extasie doth unperplex
> (We said) and tell us what we love. . . .

This strange new state of two souls 'interinanimated' by love and become a single soul 'abler' than was either alone, 'defects of lonelinesse controules' (i.e. supplies whatever is lacking in either single soul) and enables the lovers, whose souls are their real selves as Plato would have agreed, to understand where previously they were perplexed.

But (and here only, at the end of the poem, does an ironical note enter), though love's mystery lives in the soul yet 'the body is his booke': only through and in the body can 'weake men' actually *see* love manifested. Even 'true lovers' must descend to 'affections and to faculties . . . else a great Prince in prison lies': i.e. only if two bodies first come together can love's mystery have a chance to reveal itself in the union of two souls. The first part of the poem is indeed 'a dialogue of one'. There is a directness of line, an unhampered flow of the thought, which comes only when a major poet is absorbed in a major statement. Yet, at the end, char-acteristically, Donne seems almost to apologize for his metaphysical flight. The whole concept, he points out, is an imaginary one: if some other lover watches our souls return from their ecstasy to their bodies, he will see 'small change'. Yet that ironical ending works both ways, to the poem's advantage. An observer will see 'small change, when we are to bodies gone', both because we never 'really', only 'ideally', left our bodies, and because our souls are the real we, after all; although the 'dialogue of one' is now over, the timeless realization of love's mystery goes on for ever in the minds of 'pure lovers'. We have purified love, we have seen and proclaimed the truth, whatever return to the body is necessary now or in the future. The passion and certainty of *The Extasie* make it one of Donne's greatest poems. At the same time, the realistic 'earthing' of the poem's metaphysic which takes place at the end, makes it one of the most metaphysical (in the literary sense) of all his poems. The most brilliant and profound imaginative concept may seem absurd and meaningless if it is not able to 'return to the body', to relate itself at a moment's notice and without too much regret, to the material world which is most people's only 'book'. The soul is really more important, but one must also be able to look at it in such a way that it does not seem so.

No poem in *Songs and Sonets* is more metaphysical than the elaborate and magnificent *Nocturnall upon S. Lucies Day: being the shortest day*, in which Donne's subject is spiritual death, expressed in the equation of the poet (who physically survives in that he can see and analyse the state of his despair in the mirror of a dead, midwinter world) with 'nothingnesse'. 'I am None', 'I am every dead thing', 'I am their Epitaph', 'I am rebegot of absence, darknesse, death, things which are not'— throughout the poem, the poet speaks on behalf of that shrunk life of a December afternoon to which his psychological state corresponds. But human nothingness transcends nature's, because man, unlike nature, has a rational and articulate soul. In nature, love brings

life to a dead world every spring, until by the spreading
of love through the world life flourishes again in the
summer. But the poet drew his life from his love, and
found strength only in her. Now she is dead: and he
returns to that nothingness in which the solitary soul
exists before love finds it, and from which their love
had rescued him. But the new nothingness is the worse
because of knowledge, i.e. because he knows that only
love can rescue a man from it (love is spring, nothingness
is winter, the unfertile season) and knows, too, that
love for him is over. His love is dead, 'nor will my
Sunne renew', so there is no spring for him again. Hence
the poet addresses those lovers whose spring and summer
(i.e. whose love-affairs) are still before them.

This poem has echoes of *A Valediction: of weeping* in
the description of the lover's tears

> Oft a flood
> Have wee two wept, and so
> Drownd the whole world, us two;

and in the suggestion, so constantly put forward in
Donne's writings, that mutual love is a change of two
separate souls into a single whole, two hemispheres into
a single, all-embracing world, there are echoes not only
of *The Extasie* but of *The Dissolution*—

> Shee'is dead; And all which die
> To their first Elements resolve;
> And wee were mutuall Elements to us,
> And made of one another.

—and of *The Good-morrow*:

> Let sea-discoverers to new worlds have gone,
> Let Maps to other, worlds on worlds have showne,
> Let us possesse one world, each hath one, and is one.
> My face in thine eye, thine in mine appeares,
> And true plain hearts doe in the faces rest,

> Where can we find two better hemispheares,
> Without sharpe North, without declining West?

—and (picking up that phrase of the lovers, 'the whole world') of *The Canonization*—the one with the famous opening 'For Godsake hold your tongue, and let me love'—where the *leitmotiv* of the macrocosm epitomized in the microcosm of the two lovers occurs in the last verse (with its characteristic mirror image):

> You, to whom love was peace, that now is rage;
> Who did the whole worlds soule contract, and drove
> Into the glasses of your eyes
> So made such mirrors, and such spies,
> That they did all to you epitomize,
> Countries, Townes, Courts. . . .

This is indeed the sum of Donne's sexual metaphysics, that the really valid and complete relationship between man and woman fuses their souls into a perfect whole, a microcosm of a living world, that

> hath no decay;
> This, no to morrow hath, nor yesterday,
> Running it never runs from us away,
> But truly keepes his first, last, everlasting day.
> (*The Anniversarie*, 7–10)

And despair is the mirror of the soul divided again by loss of love. A divided world is a world of nothingness, full of the 'defects of loneliness'. A man who has never experienced, and a man who has through death lost, his love, is 'ruined'. Although Donne speaks sometimes (e.g. in *The Anniversarie*) of love transcending the grave, we cannot so defy his whole philosophy as to suppose he means that life hereafter is a continuation of life on earth. Love is essentially a youthful and humanistic creed, the answer to happiness here on earth, the lifeline of the 'rebel and atheist' that was Donne in his youth and which is most of us throughout our lives. In his later years, his mind, as he himself said, wholly set on heavenly things, Donne wrote of his love for God: but he wrote still of a supreme experience of *this* life, of something essentially human, fallible and not transcendental.

In connexion with the *Nocturnall*, which analysed the perpetual despair of the lover whose love death has destroyed, we should also consider *Twicknam Garden*, in which, as in the *Nocturnall*, the forsaken lover speaks to lovers who have not yet experienced his desolation. But here it is not death but woman's inconstancy which causes the poet's torment, and the treatment is, accordingly, closer to the surface of ordinary experience: the colour not black, but grey. Petulance and a sardonic gloom here enter, where in the *Nocturnall* was only a less fanciful and more final darkness. If the *Nocturnall* is Donne's finest metaphysical treatment of permanent division, permanent separation, permanent lovelessness, *Twicknam Garden* is certainly his finest metaphysical treatment of temporary division, temporary separation, temporary lovelessness. In the *Nocturnall*, the wheel had come full circle and brought complete resignation: in *Twicknam Garden*, the wheel is stuck half-way round, and, the fancied situation being of lesser gravity, the response is one of self-pity. Donne here indulges in an orgy of tears. They start in the first line, with its four strong, irregularly placed stresses

> Blasted with sighs, and surrounded with teares,

and this world of weeping is gradually explored until in the last verse a more precise statement emerges, a (literal) 'testing' of the tears:

> Hither with christall vyals, lovers come,
> And take my teares, which are loves wine,

> And try your mistresse Teares at home,
> For all are false, that tast not just like mine;

Tears had an obsessional value as imagery to Donne, who, like all Elizabethans, sometimes wore his heart on his sleeve. They represented worlds of genuine grief— his own tears, and also the easy physical simulation of grief—the mistress's tears. This ambivalence also appeared in *A Valediction: of weeping*.

The difference of mood between this poem and the *Nocturnall* is inherent in their difference of season: in *Twicknam Garden*, the season is spring and summer, and it is the contrast between the smiling face of Nature and the poet's dark gloom which gives the poem some of its effect; just as, in the much profounder annihilation of the *Nocturnall*, Nature and all created things are lying in winter's dead dark, yet

> seeme to laughe
> Compar'd with mee who am their Epitaph.

In the *Nocturnall* Donne could welcome the sympathies of winter and yet, in his superior human capacity for experience and articulate suffering, could also 'go one better', or rather one worse, in knowing and saying that the natural world would be reborn with the spring, while he would not. But it is altogether on a much more superficial and conventionally poetic level of fanciful expostulation that the poet of *Twicknam Garden* chides the garden for being a Paradise:

> 'Twere wholsomer for mee, that winter did
> Benight the glory of this place,
> And that a grave frost did forbid
> These trees to laugh, and mocke mee to my face;

This is sheer 'conceit-writing' and of a relatively simple kind: the poet chiding natural phenomena for failing to respond to the key of his human sadness is a familiar poetic spectacle. Donne·treats it in his own personal and trenchant idiom, but it is essentially no different from a hundred other such laments. We can find it in medieval Latin and Italian, and in these lines of the Earl of Surrey (*d.* 1547):

> The soote season, that bud and bloom forth brings
> With green hath clad the hill and eke the vale . . .
> And thus I see among those pleasant things
> Each care decays, and yet my sorrow springs.

As for Donne's

> spider love, which transubstantiates all,
> And can convert Manna to gall

we may compare Leontes in *The Winter's Tale*, jealous and disillusioned:

> I have drunk, and seen the spider.

Donne's most characteristic conceit in this poem is his desire to be 'some senslesse peece of this place' like the plants and stones of the *Nocturnall*, which can love and hate in rudimentary fashion according to medieval philosophy's hierarchy and classification of the soul-value of all created objects—the 'ordinary nothings'—

> or a stone fountaine weeping out my yeare.

The climax of the poem undoubtedly comes in the working out of the poet's desire to put off human misery and yet retain human experience. Let the lovers draw off water from the fountain which was the poet, and they will draw off genuine tears, by which they can try (i.e. test) their

> mistresse Teares at home,
> For all are false, that tast not just like mine.

That is a wonderful line: and Donne saves most of his

poems, including some less good than the present, with such lines.

The more one reads Donne's poems, especially the *Songs and Sonets*, the more one sees the folly of over-classification. Each poem captures a unique mood, though maybe a mood only slightly different from that captured in a poem on a similar theme—just as Cézanne spent hours, under a changing light, painting the same tree, on the ground that one tree was after all very like another and that what mattered, and what altered, was the tree's relationship with that changing light, the angles from which it could be painted, and the changing moods these changing relationships engendered in the sensibility of the artist who tried to set them down. What the tree was to Cézanne, love is to Donne. Sometimes he sees the tormented artist at rest in a mystical immortality, and the loved one as the very soul of the world:

> But yet thou canst not die, I know;
> To leave this world behinde, is death,
> But when thou from this world wilt goe,
> The whole world vapors with thy breath.
>
> Or if, when thou, the worlds soule, goest,
> It stay, 'tis but thy carkasse then . . .
>
> *(A Feaver, 5–10)*

Sometimes it is the concrete components and manifestations of love which he analyses; especially the tears of love, and the hearts of lovers. In *Lovers Infiniteness*, one of his most beautiful and gentle poems,

> If yet I have not all thy love,
> Deare, I shall never have it all,

he transmutes metaphysical speculations on the meanings of the phrase 'all thy love' into a most musical and extraordinarily *easy* and lucid song. The poem illustrates

well the basis of all Renaissance poetic technique, which
is an awareness of, and interest in, the many possible
meanings and associations of words arranged in a logical
pattern. At its worst, the technique interests by its
ingenuity: at its best, it is capable of tremendous things,
simply because it can gather into one so many different
possibilities, and can, without destroying any one of
them, yet create something which adds up to more than
all of them. If 'all your love' means 'all the love I can
persuade you to give me', then, says the poet, either I
must have it now or I shall never have it: for I have no
means of eliciting love which I have not already employed.
Again, if 'all your love' means 'all the love you were
capable of when you first declared you loved me', then
perhaps there are new feelings inspired in you since
then by other men; if so, I should still claim them, for
you gave me your heart and 'all your love' must mean
that, so that all new passions that your heart engenders
are mine. But this is word-play:

> Thou canst not every day give me thy heart,
> If thou canst give it, then thou never gavest it:
> Loves riddles are, that though thy heart depart,
> It stayes at home, and thou with losing savest it:
> But wee will have a way more liberall,
> Then changing hearts, to joyne them, so wee shall
> Be one, and one anothers All.

How disarmingly does that phrase 'Loves riddles' seem
to mock at all that the poet up till then has been saying.
The ending seems almost trite, but the last line of all is
charged with all the disputed and reconciled meanings
of the poem, and provides a perfect coda. The poem is
indeed 'made with words': there is nothing concrete
held up to the light: over no real tear does the poet
pause, and even the word 'heart' is but a word, although
one of the supercharged ones in the language. Such a

poem is a musical offering, of course: but it is also a piece of verbal sophistication, and verbal sophistication (in the fullest sense of the phrase) lies often at the heart of Donne's most impassioned outbursts. Tricks with ideas, so far as poetry is concerned, are tricks with words; we have seen how the word 'heart' is 'expounded' in the last verse of this poem; we saw it in other guises in *The Legacie*, but still it was a word:

> But oh, no man could hold it, for twas thine.

And in *The Broken Heart*:

> Ah, what a trifle is a heart,
> If once into loves hands it come!

it is as if Donne is picking up this most hallowed emblem of love-poetry, picking it up, say, where Sidney left it in that famous poem, 'My true love hath my heart and I have his', and holding it like a shell to our ears, so that it 're-echoes, thus, in our minds'.

In Sidney the word is constant and limited: constant, in that its implications do not change with repetition of the word; limited, in that those implications are defined by a long tradition of the poetry of courtly love: it is the very 'heart' of every serenade. And indeed there is surely a deliberate reply to Sidney intended by Donne in that last verse, quoted above, of *Lovers Infiniteness*. Sidney's heart ends as it began: the last line of his poem is the same as the first. Donne's uses of the word are neither constant nor limited:

> Yet I found something like a heart.

No Elizabethan sonneteer could have used the word so; and in *The Legacie*, by using that strange concrete imagery —belonging, not to the world of the traditional school-exercise rhetorical 'topic', but to the violent, melo-dramatic world of the plays of Donne's contemporaries

Webster and Tourneur—of the dead man's ghost plunging its hands into its own corpse to try to pluck the heart out, we are reminded, with a jolt, that to Donne the word heart meant all that Sidney meant, but also meant what it meant to a butcher or a surgeon, and meant more than the sum of those meanings. Let us pursue the word into another of the *Songs and Sonets*: *The Blossome*. The flower on the tree has its brief hour of sunshine and glory, then falls and disintegrates, when the branch withers. The poet's heart seeks the sunshine and security of a lodgment in his body while it is near to his mistress and to love. But—and throughout the poem the heart is apostrophized and endowed with speech—the poet's body will go away, and physically, therefore, the heart cannot stay behind with the woman. 'Why not?' asks the heart: 'my function is (technically speaking) love: you take your body and senses and tongue to London and do your business without me.' 'All right', replies the poet. 'But she won't thank you if you stay, nor even recognize

A naked thinking heart, that makes no show.

Take my word,' says the poet, 'she doth not know a heart.' The ending of the poem is, like the rest of it, perverse and tender at once. But it well represents part of what must be reckoned with under the heading 'metaphysical': starting from the idea, the 'topic', that if one leaves one's mistress one's sentimental part wishes to stay, i.e. one's thoughts and feelings linger with her, Donne expresses this by letting 'heart' (the word fullest in associations of an amatory kind) stand literally for the sentimental part, and taking the logical consequences: like the tear seen as a global map, this sort of conceit produces results which may disconcert anyone who thought a word in a poem had only one meaning. By 'delimiting' the word 'heart' to stand for the idea I have just stated, Donne is able to enlarge our experience of the power to suggest of common words: for 'heart' brings with it into this poem the simple, single, conventional meaning it has in Sidney's poem, and takes in addition a new and unexpected set of meanings. The word is dragged away from its simple traditional sonneteer's isolation and made to compete with

> eyes, eares, and tongue, and every part.

Indeed the heart in simple, touching, sentimental isolation is cleverly dismissed as an unreality, a convention—

> A naked thinking heart, that makes no show
> Is to a woman, but a kinde of Ghost,

—something which a woman in reality 'doth not know'. Even in *Lovers Infiniteness*, the heart is made rich by the idea expressed in the poem's last lines (of the completeness and totality of their love); even though that finale is in itself no very new thing, the verbal consummation with which the verbal fancies are crowned makes those very fancies more vigorous and compelling because leading to a statement of emotional importance. As for *The Broken Heart*, the adjective of the title is far from limited or idealized in its significance:

> love, alas,
> At one first blow did shiver it as glass.

This 'heart' is something which can be brought into a room and be smashed like a glass: Donne says so. In *The Legacie* he found no simple cloudy denomination of true love, but

> something like a heart,

while in that sad and elegant little poem *The Message* harping again on the idea (seen in *The Legacie*) of the

John Donne, aged about 44

A portrait of John Donne in his shroud
from the frontispiece to Deaths Duell *1632*

poet in love 'giving his heart', the false mistress is supposed, while the heart is in her possession, to make it as false as her own: if this be so, says Donne, do not send back my heart but

> Keepe it, for then 'tis none of mine.

And, to take one further example, in *The Dampe*, one of those poems in which Donne imagines himself dead (of love-sickness: a damp was a sort of stupor or trance), the heart appears both anatomically (as in *The Legacie*) and at the same time metaphorically, thus:

> When I am dead, and Doctors know not why,
>   And my friends curiositie
> Will have me cut up to survay each part,
> When they shall find your Picture in my heart. . . .

We have seen how the love-relationship is expressed in many of those poems as the way of creating a complete world. Sometimes this seems almost a declaration of solipsism on the part of Donne, as for example in *The Sunne Rising*, where it is categorically stated that

> She'is all States and all Princes, I,
>   Nothing else is,

and where the sun, in allusion to Ovid, is told,

> Thy beames, so reverend, and strong
> Why shouldst thou thinke?
> I could eclipse and cloud 'them with a winke,
> But that I would not lose her sight so long:
> . . . Thine age askes ease, and since thy duties bee
> To warme the world, that's done in warming us.
> Shine here to us, and thou art every where;
> This bed thy center is, these walls, thy sphaere.

This poem (with its reference to 'both the Indias') is perhaps an ironic echo of Spenser's fifteenth sonnet. The *Songs and Sonets* and the *Elegies* are a new-found-land, a

G

late sixteenth-century voyage of literary discovery: dramatic lyrics, moving away from song towards speech: a private rhetoric in which an extraordinary mind discusses many of the ideas and moods which were also beginning to dominate English drama about the year 1600.

In Shakespeare's *Richard II*, produced in 1595, before Donne was twenty-five, the doomed King has a famous speech of philosophic self-consolation:

> I have been studying how I may compare
> This prison where I live unto the world,
> And for because the world is populous
> And here is not a creature but myself
> I cannot do it; yet I'll hammer't out.
> My brain I'll prove the female to my soul,
> My soul the father: and these two beget
> A generation of still-breeding thoughts,
> And these same thoughts people this little world.
>
> (Act v. sc. 5)

'I cannot do it: yet I'll hammer't out': Donne went further. He could do it, as Shakespeare later did it also, without hammering, with the boldest and most brilliant of dramatic ellipses. This passage is, as it were, metaphysical verse with the scaffolding still there; Richard is learning, too late, to think and analyse and compare:

> I wasted time, and now doth time waste me.

Much metaphysical poetry depends on a vivid and often elliptical use of the device of metaphor, extended, by means of a basic philosophy which links the whole of the created universe, into the device, primarily philosophical not poetical, of *analogy*. The tear that, in *A Valediction: of weeping*, becomes a coin and then a world is offered analogously rather than metaphorically; but when 'our two soules' in *A Valediction: forbidding mourning* are described as 'stiffe twin compasses', a metaphor, culled not from any traditional poetic but from mathematics, is worked out—not 'hammered out' like Richard's metaphors, but delineated with complete 'correspondencie'. Donne of course was professionally trained, as a Catholic theologian and lawyer, in all the complexities of medieval scholastic philosophy, and this is what gives his verse its special technical and intellectual characteristics. His successors dug deep for them, often lacking the natural inclination to think as Donne did. But it was Donne's natural way of expressing himself, the method perfectly suited to his temperament.

Coleridge spoke of the casual, decorative impulse of 'fancy' and contrasted it with the unifying creative reconciling power of 'imagination'. Metaphysical poetry at its most 'obvious' and flamboyant is often fanciful. Thus in the early poems of Milton we find 'conceits' such as the metaphysical poets revel in:

> So when the Sun in bed,
> Curtained with cloudy red,
>   Pillows his chin upon an Orient wave
>   (*On the Morning of Christ's Nativity*, 229–31)

This is 'wit-writing'; but it is not such 'fancies', that stick out like plums in a cake, which are really important in Donne. Wit is also a quality of the imagination, and it is in the imagination that it takes wings and becomes an instrument to be reckoned with in creating new images which are enduring and significant enough to modify our views on the very nature of the poetic experience. Donne set no limit to the places he would search for his material: but over all his choices he threw the cloak of his unique personality. His imagery is rarely as universal or as deep-rooted as Shakespeare's in ordinary experience. And of course in his lyrics he wrote for no audience, had none to please: these were not for patrons but for himself and he had no reason to expect that in them he was in communication with more than a few other minds. He puzzles and disconcerts too much to be really popular as a poet: combining sonorous and startling splendour of imagery, in the same poem, with abstract and elliptical word-play. His most powerful imagery is concerned with the attributes and sensations of love (physical and metaphysical, passion and ecstasy, sighs, tears, hearts and mystical oneness) or with death, particularly death as separation from love. Yet his mordant and fanciful wit draws on every branch of contemporary knowledge and life, from particular techniques like falconry

> Thus I reclaim'd my buzard love, to flye
> At what, and when, and how, and where I chuse;
>   Now negligent of sport I lye,
>   And now as other Fawkners use,
> I spring a mistresse, sweare, write, sigh and weepe:
> And the game kill'd, or lost, goe talke, and sleepe.
>
> *(Loves Diet, 25–30)*

(a perfect instance, incidentally, of Donne at his most conversational and 'natural': casual, extremely intimate as these observations are, they are yet organized on an image of great technical exactness so that there is a logical analogy connecting the series of off-hand remarks) to the whole field of Renaissance scholarship and learning, of which the best example is *A Valediction: of the Booke*, containing allusions to, or mentions of, the Sibyl, Pindar, Lucan, Homer, theology, cryptography, Platonic philosophy, lawyers, statesmen, the Bible, alchemy and astronomy.

Donne in his lyrics borrows many of the tricks and some of the material formerly reserved for satire, thus innovat-

ing to a remarkable degree: the lyric in his hands is extended to cover a wider and subtler range of expression.
He left the English lyric capable, perhaps, of too much,
and ready to degenerate in the hands of the verbose. The
history of the lyric, after Donne's death, is largely the
story of, on the one hand, his influence towards wit,
startling innovation of imagery, variety of theme and
mood, realism of treatment combined with an intellectual approach to the psychology of a situation; and on the
other hand, his friend Ben Jonson's influence towards the
classical, marmoreal dignity of the traditional, formal
lyric, with its more restricted and more closely defined
code of possibilities. But in Donne's lyrics, the rhetorical and the ratiocinative, the emotional and the argu-
mentative, the learned and the casual, the conversational and the philosophical, fall into as many different
patterns, with as many different tones and attitudes as
there are poems. That is why generalizations and
classifications are so difficult. Fortunately, there is no
need to try and sum up the *Songs and Sonets*: Donne has
done it for us, in these superb stanzas from *A Valediction: of the Booke*

> This Booke, as long-liv'd as the elements,
>   Or as the worlds forme, this all-graved tome
>   In cypher writ, or new made Idiome.
> Wee for loves clergie only'are instruments:
>   When this booke is made thus,
>   Should againe the ravenous
>   Vandals and Goths inundate us,
>   Learning were safe; in this our Universe
> Schooles might learne Sciences, Spheares Musick, Angels
>   Verse.
>
> Here Loves Divines (since all Divinity
>   Is love or wonder) may find all they seeke,
>   Whether abstract spirituall love they like,

Their soules exhal'd with what they do not see,
    Or, loth so to amuze
    Faiths infirmitie, they chuse
    Something which they may see and use;
    For, though minde be the heaven, where love doth sit,
Beauty a convenient type may be to figure it.

2. ELEGIES

The twenty poems called *Elegies*, first published together in 1633, are varied in depth and content, and
united only by their generic title and their metre, the
couplets in which the satires, the *Anniversaries* and most
of the verse-letters are also written—the standard metre
for 'occasional' verse. The elegy, though Greek in
origin, may be for practical purposes regarded as a
Roman invention, its great master being the fashionable
Augustan poet Ovid, writing of the town for the town.
His poems, an elegant mixture of wit, pathos, conventional indecency and digestible erudition, were highly
popular as models of form and style throughout the
Middle Ages and the Renaissance. Only with the final
collapse of the old Europe, at the close of the eighteenth
century, did their popularity wane. Now they are still
less widely read than the poems of Horace, Lucretius
and Virgil which have a more personal, romantic appeal,
although there are signs of an Ovid revival at last.

Donne's *Elegies*, like Ovid's, are the product of an
urban culture which has not yet reacted wholeheartedly
against the traditional values of courtly love, and the style
of a good half of them is closer to satire than to such
elegies as Gray's or *Lycidas* or *Adonais*. Though undated,
many of them are clearly early pieces written in the
1590's. A glance at some of their titles will provide
some guide to their nature: *Jealousie*, *The Anagram*,

Change, The Perfume, His Picture, On His Mistress, Variety, Going to Bed, Loves Progress, Loves Warre (this last is a purely Ovidian idea: 'militat omnis amans'). Their characteristics are, vigour, concrete imagery, a set of psychological attitudes found also in some of the more 'cynical' of the *Songs and Sonets*, and a particular conventional morality or rather amorality proper to this form of literary exercise (all husbands should be cuckolded, all women are fickle) which expresses itself in the confident artificiality of the situations employed. Most of these features, except the racy and masterful use of language, which is purely Donne's, and which is the sole reason we read the poems, were inherited from Ovid.

The first elegy may be analysed as an example: 'Your husband is jealous of us, so we should be grateful and kind to the poor old man for warning us to be careful: from now on we will not "kiss and play in his house as before" but in another house.' This theme is worked out through a metaphysical analogy which runs like this: 'Silly girl, why look so sad because your husband is jealous? If he were dying, you'd not weep, but be jolly: so why weep now, when you see him killing himself with jealousy? That spells for you as happy a release as would his actual death, since we will be warned no longer to risk his "household policies"[1] by cuckolding him in his own house.' The language of the poem is raucous, thudding, concrete and graphic:

> If swolne with poyson, hee lay in' his last bed,
> . . . Drawing his breath, as thick and short, as can
> The nimblest crotcheting Musitian,
> Ready with loathsome vomiting to spue
> His Soule out of one hell, into a new. . . .

Much of the language of the *Elegies* involves contemporary allusions: this type of verse, like satire, can hold

[1] i.e. tricks.

a cracked mirror up to nature. Sometimes these allusions enable us to date an elegy: the fourteenth, for instance, *A Tale of a Citizen and his Wife*, contains references to 'the Virginian plot' (a plan to colonize Virginia) and 'new-built Algate' (Aldgate), both of which events belong to the year 1609. This fourteenth elegy is an interesting and amusing one: it is in the style of Horace's 'Sermones' or conversation-pieces, a kind of satirical verse-letter, but addressed to no one in particular, recounting the sort of incident that would make a funny story in the club. The poet meets a citizen and his wife, the latter pretty and giving (and getting) the glad eye. The citizen is pleasantly hit off as a comfortable, pompous bore, a *laudator temporis acti*: 'for he gave no praise/To any but my lord of Essex dayes/Called those the age of action'; he takes no interest in contemporary events with which Donne tries to draw him. At last they reach an inn, where

> I pray'd him stay,
> To take some due refreshment by the way.

But the citizen

> refus'd and made away,
> Though willing she pleaded a weary day:

whereupon, says the poet,

> I found my misse, struck hands, and praid him tell
> (To hold acquaintance still) where he did dwell;
> He barely nam'd the street, promis'd the Wine,
> But his kinde wife gave me the very Signe.

Even those elegies which go deeper emotionally, and strike us with greater force, are often still on that sort of level: for instance, the famous *Going to Bed* (XIX) describes exactly what its title indicates. It is addressed by the poet to his mistress, and the celebrated expostulation (with its pun on 'discovering')

> Licence my roaving hands, and let them go,
> Before, behind, between, above, below.
> O my America! my new-found-land,
> My kingdome, safeliest when with one man man'd,
> My Myne of precious stones, My Empery,
> How blest am I in this discovering thee!

is a fine piece of wit-writing. Donne's analogy is from Elizabethan navigation and discovery, by which means he depicts the lover's journey to consummation in the most modern possible fashion. The same sort of witty effect is often to be found in love-poetry of the poets of the so-called 'pylon' school in the 1930's. Donne neatly hits (and 'takes') off the traditional estimate of love by expressing it in terms of an adventure which, if you are not a metaphysical poet, you will never have thought of associating with love. An Elizabethan explorer, with traditional ideas about keeping poetry in its proper place, might have thought the conceit absurd and unfitting. A rake who had never been out of London might have been delighted by the comparison even as he reflected wryly upon the implication that, if *this* is all there is in discovery, then man is easily fooled into romanticizing his own achievements, and the voyage to America, so far from being difficult, can be made any night. The idea of the world of the lover and the world of the voyager is used often, and with varying intention and subtlety, by Donne, but nowhere more shamelessly than here. The tone of this nineteenth elegy is in any case unmistakeably established by the opening couplet with its witty, punning impatience

> Come, Madam, come, all rest my powers defie,
> Until I labour, I in labour lie

and sustained right up to the matching final couplet

> To teach thee, I am naked first; why than
> What needst thou have more covering than a man.

Beautiful indeed are many of the lines of the poem, but
the mock-heroic imagery cannot have deceived its first
readers. In an age when style had to match substance,
such a poem could not have been taken on a level higher
than that of its last two lines. Beautiful, after all, are
occasional lines throughout the *Elegies*: sometimes the
formal Elizabethan beauty which the metre will not with-
hold even from so forceful a user of it as Donne: for
example, in XVII—

> The sun that sitting in the chaire of light
> Sheds flame into what else so ever doth seem bright,

—the alexandrine protracts the flood of light which
dazzles and dominates this poem; or, again, in the same
elegy,

> The last I saw in all extreames is faire,
> And holds me in the Sun-beames of her haire;

In this poem, and others, particularly No. XII, *His
parting from Her*, we find an antithetical handling of the
couplet for ends which, as in the eighteenth century, are
most effective when they are most sophisticated. This
witty, antithetical manner is natural to the couplet, and
can be found constantly in the Elizabethans' handling of
it: a good example is Iago's witty set-piece about women
(a natural 'couplet' theme) in *Othello*, II, 1.

This twelfth elegy is very different, in mood, tone and
attitude, from the rough, juvenile first elegy. The
opening is in a dark key:

> Since she must go, and I must mourn, come Night,
> Environ me with darkness, whilst I write:
> Shadow that hell unto me, which alone
> I am to suffer when my Love is gone.
> Alas the darkest Magick cannot do it,
> Thou and great Hell to boot are shadows to it.
> Should *Cinthia* quit thee, *Venus*, and each starre,

> It would not forme one thought dark as mine are.
> I could lend thee obscureness now, and say,
> Out of myself, There should be no more Day.

And yet, further on in this impressive nocturne, we realize—with perhaps something of a shock—that the convention within which the poet is writing, the standpoint from which this outpouring stems, is still supposed to be none other than that of the first elegy, the standpoint of the adulterous lover, the mock-romantic Ovidian 'hero': but now he speaks with a passion and purpose that increases as the poem presses on:

> Was't not enough, that thou didst hazard us
> To paths in love so dark, so dangerous:
> And those so ambush'd round with household spies,
> And over all thy husbands towering eyes
> That flam'd with oylie sweat of jealousy.

It is the same situation as in the first elegy: that last line, indeed, speaks the same resentful, contemptuous language; but the husband here is taken more seriously, with his towering eyes. What before was only a game is here a genuine experience. The poet has intensified his material, perhaps out of his own experience: the atmosphere of darkness established in lines one to ten catches us up again at the repetition of 'dark' in

> To paths in love so dark, so dangerous

and persuades us that, this time, the jealous husband is no mere figure of (or in) farce, but a serious element in a situation considerably felt by the poet. The poetic figuration of *this* lover in *this* situation is of course finer, and more involved *in* the situation, than the lover in elegy I, and Donne is master of a finer poetic instrument. The daytime, *ad hoc* elements of the Ovidian-Elizabethan satiric elegy are fused in a nocturnal love-poem of a sort which is uniquely Donne's. The poet-lover, here, swears eternal love in some of the finest closing lines to be found in Elizabethan elegy:

> For this to th' comfort of my Dear I vow,
> My Deeds shall still be what my words are now;
> The Poles shall move to teach me ere I start;
> And when I change my Love, I'll change my heart;
> Nay, if I wax but cold in my desire,
> Think, heaven hath motion lost, and the world, fire:
> Much more I could, but many words have made
> That, oft, suspected which men would perswade:
> Take therefore all in this: I love so true,
> As I will never look for less in you.

Donne wishes this speaker to be believed: the elemental imagery gives solemnity and permanence to a situation more often expressed on a lower level. Here, the lover remains on the classical heights of the true artificer:

> I will not look upon the quickning Sun,
> But straight her beauty to my sense shall run;
> The ayre shall note her soft, the fire most pure;
> Water suggest her Dear, and the earth sure.
> Time shall not lose our passages; the Spring
> How fresh our love was in the beginning;
> The Summer, how it ripened in the eare;
> And Autumn, what our golden harvests were.

That passage seems to me to exemplify Donne's use of natural description (elements, seasons, etc.) to illuminate some aspect of man (or woman): he is rarely interested in natural phenomena for their own sake.

Elegy XVI, *On his mistris*, has sometimes been read as a chapter of autobiography. If we cannot, on the strength of 'by thy father's wrath', name Ann as the subject of the poem, we can suppose that she, and Sir George More, suggested the lines. The theme of the elegy is that the mistress would disguise as a boy in order to go abroad with her lover. Such a course *may*

have been (though it seems unlikely) considered by
Donne and Ann; what is more likely is that the poem is a
conflation of ideas and details suggested to Donne by
the difficulties of his courtship and the opposition of
Sir George More, by a later occasion when Donne
actually did leave Ann, after their marriage, to go abroad
(perhaps the journey of 1611, when we know Ann to
have been nervous of separation), and by literary sources.
The *idea* is not original: it is the poem's personal tone,
and certain details probably the result of actual experience,
which make it much more than a literary exercise on
a set theme. No one can help being moved by the slow,
serious opening lines

> By our first strange and fatall interview,
> By all desires which thereof did ensue,
> By our long starving hopes. . . .

which go on their measured way, piling up clauses like
pleas. Equally remarkable is the curiously vivid,
realistic glimpse into the future as the mistress's fears
imagine it, when the poet begs her not to let herself
panic when he is away:

> nor in bed fright thy Nurse
> With midnights startings, crying out, oh, oh
> Nurse, oh my love is slaine, I saw him goe
> O'r the white Alpes alone; I saw him I,
> Assail'd, fight, taken, stabb'd, bleed, fall, and die.

The dramatic suddenness of the girl's cry to her nurse is
reminiscent of one of those stabbing felicites of Webster.
The piled-up, monosyllabic verbs occur elsewhere in
Donne: in the elegies, again, at No. XX, 30, 'here
let mee parley, batter, bleed and die', and in the Holy
Sonnets. This passage, however, is, as a whole, curious
and interesting; beneath the force of the glimpsed,
distant possibility, the poet speaks smilingly, chiding and

comforting: the girl is asked not to imagine a scene which is one of the poet's most intensely imagined.

Elegy IX, *The Autumnall*, I have already referred to in the first chapter: it is one of the best of those elegies which fall into a courtly, 'occasional' tradition of poems for patrons. It is addressed to a real woman, not to the usual 'mistress' of the elegiac poet: in that sense it is, indeed, easier to consider it a verse-letter. Elegy VIII, on the other hand, *The Comparison*, is one of the most notorious of the 'elegies rampant', a crude, brilliant study in insult by paradox, turning the conventional praise of women inside out, as Shakespeare did in his sonnet 'My mistress' eyes are nothing like the sun' but going much further, with such exuberances as 'spermatique issue of ripe menstruous boils'. It is a *tour de force*, and so is Elegy II, *The Anagram*, which is typical Donne:

> Though all her parts be not in th' usuall place,
> She'hath yet an Anagram of a good face

is very good comic writing.

3. SATIRES

> Quidquid agunt homines, votum timor ira voluptas
> Gaudia discursus, nostri farrago libelli est.

'Whatever men do, their prayers, fear, anger, pleasure, their joys, their distractions—of all these is my book a medley.' So Juvenal defined the scope of satire, a form of poetry virtually invented by the Romans. As will be seen, the definition is a comprehensive one. Perhaps Juvenal's great predecessor Horace might have added charm to the list, but Horace had no successor, and though 'imitated' by Pope, he is inimitable. Elizabethan satire followed the more representative and more easily affected harshness and obscurity of Persius and his successor Juvenal. Their poems were avowed assaults on vice. Their idiom is concrete and their standpoint that of the upholder of old-fashioned virtue against a degenerating mankind. They took as their subjects and their victims a corrupt Imperial Roman society, which offered them a good choice of material: *quidquid agunt homines*, in fact. Their manner, and this is what interests us, was discursive, anecdotal and allusive: concrete examples, presented with the maximum of colourful and realistic detail, mingle with passages of philosophical generalization on the fallen nature of man and the decadence and rottenness of the times—passages beloved as *loci classici* by generations of medieval schoolmen, and thereafter perpetuated as tags by further generations of the classically-educated. The metre, though nominally the standard Latin hexameter, has none of the melli-fluity of Ovid or the refined and subtle variety of Virgil. It is rough, breaks the rules when it likes, can bring off, every now and then, a resounding rhetorical line, but is often over-crammed, difficult and tedious. The writing of satire in this tradition became suddenly very popular in England at the end of the sixteenth century. It allowed criticism of contemporary morals, manners and policies, which might be partly genuine, partly opportunism.

Donne's five satires were among the earliest written at this time. They probably belong to the years 1593–1598. They are modelled in style and technique on Persius and, like Roman satire (which could only have been called forth by the evils attendant upon life in Rome), they are thoroughly metropolitan in spirit and belong naturally to Jack Donne's early days as a London law-student.

> Sir; though (I thanke God for it) I do hate
> Perfectly all this towne. . . .

One can't be urbane without being urban, and satire is a form of private tragi-comedy, sociably anti-social. The satirist must appear as a *poseur*, taking up an attitude of moral and intellectual superiority, to carry off which one needs a large vocabulary, a short range (i.e. a few choice spirits among whom to circulate one's efforts) and the rhetorician's rather than the lyric poet's technique.

It is not surprising that Donne's satires are very uneven. One's mind is often taken by a fine and just observation, a clever example, a memorable phrase: and then one suddenly finds one has lost the thread of the often difficult argument, and is becoming bored. Only the third satire, on religion, seems wholly to have engaged Donne's personal feelings. It is here that there occur[1] those famous lines on truth which are Donne at his absolute best as a poetic craftsman. The strong, yet extraordinarily expressive blank verse is forced, by his poetic will, to *become* in its sounds and movement the meaning which, in lesser poets, blank verse merely clothes.

> On a huge hill,
> Cragged, and steep, Truth stands,

—in these slow, majestic lines truth stands out as naked as the successive Anglo-Saxon syllables which compose the lines. There is a pause, obviously, after 'truth stands', emphasizing the eternal 'thereness' of this bare and celestial mountain. Then, when we get to

> and hee that will
> Reach her, about must, and about must goe

the curious trick of rhythm induced by the position, *vis-à-vis* the iambic stresses of the metric norm, of 'about must, and about must goe', carries with it an uncanny

[1] Lines 79–84.

Anna

orgij ⎫   Mori de   ⎫   Filia
berti ⎬   Lothesley,   ⎬   Soror:
elmi   ⎮   Equit: ⎮   Nept:
istophori ⎭   Aurat: ⎭   pronept:

Fœmina lectißima, dilectißimæqᵉ
Coniugi charißima, castißimæqᵉ;
Matrj pijßima, ſᵈdulgentißimæqᵉ;
XV annis in coniugio transactis,
vii post xiiᵐ partum (quorum vii superstant) dies
    Ammam febre correpta,
(Quod hoc saxum farj iußit
    Ipse, præ dolore Infans)
Maritus (miserrimum dictu) olim chara charus
    Cmoribus cineres spondet suos
Nouo matrimonio (annuat Deus) hoc loco sociandos
    Johannes Donne
    Sacr: Theolog: profeſs:
        Secessit
Aᵒ xxxiiiᵒ Ætatis suæ et Jhũ Jesu
    CIↃ ↃC Xviiᵒ   221
    Aug: xv.

John Donne's epitaph for his wife, in his own
handwriting, 1617

*A sermon being preached at St. Paul's Cross,
before James I, 1620*

suggestion of the baffled seeker after truth; no less brilliant is the way in which 'will', by its emphatic position at the end of the line, is forced to take all the emphasis of meaning which it must have. Finally, 'the hill's suddennes resists' speeds us up with a jerk, so that we feel the traveller being brought up short by that sheer mountain-side, that verbal barrier 'resists'.

The third satire is particularly interesting when the early date of its composition is remembered. It offers, at a time when Donne's interest in religion was certainly not a professional one, a reasoned and reasonable protest again extremism and schism. Significantly, Rome is already lumped with other European churches and not accorded any special sanction:

> Seeke true religion. O where? Mirreus
> Thinking her unhous'd here, and fled from us,
> Seekes her at Rome, there, because hee doth know
> That shee was there a thousand yeares agoe.

Characteristically English in spirit, the poem rejects any absolute, permanently 'true' form of religion in favour of an empirical, relative approach:

> As women do in divers countries goe
> In divers habits, yet are still one kinde,
> So doth, so is Religion;

Such broadmindedness and open-mindedness is a clear indication of Donne's natural dislike of all intractable claims to unique truth. Two words in this satire— 'doubt wisely'—i.e. 'suspend judgment'—support the sense of the famous 'truth' passage, which from a Catholic point of view is heretical enough. The advice, in line 89, 'Keepe the truth which thou hast found', lays a thoroughly Protestant onus on the individual to make up his own mind; and later, in the peroration, the laws of God and the laws of man are sharply contrasted

H

to the discomfiture of the latter which, Donne suggests, are the canon of most dogmatic religionists.

> Foole and wretch, wilt thou let thy Soule be tyed
> To mans lawes, by which she shall not be tryed
> At the last day? O, will it then boot thee
> To say a Philip,[1] or a Gregory,[2]
> A Harry,[3] or a Martin[4] taught thee this?
> Is not this excuse for mere contraries,
> Equally strong? cannot both sides say so?
> That thou mayest rightly obey power, her bounds know;

And the final condemnation is of those who 'chuse mens unjust/Power from God claym'd' rather than 'God himselfe to trust'.

The modernity of this controversy between God's word and its differing interpreters makes the third satire the most readable and interesting of the five, and the most important in any study of Donne. Its homogeneity, its lucidity and its objectivity, and also its lack of sensationalism (religions are a good target, but do not offer the same possibilities as certain other human weaknesses), make it far less Juvenalian, far less of a 'farrago', than, say, the first two satires, which run much more to type.

The first satire, on London society, takes us into the sort of rip-roaring, cut-and-thrust, allusive atmosphere in which satire normally kicks and thrives:

> Now leaps he upright, Joggs me, and cryes, Do you see
> Yonder well favoured youth? Which? Oh, 'tis hee
> That dances so divinely; Oh, said I,
> Stand still, must you dance here for company?
> Hee droopt, wee went, till one (which did excell
> Th' Indians, in drinking his Tobacco well)

[1] Of Spain.
[2] Pope Gregory, probably XIII or XIV.
[3] Henry VIII.
[4] Luther.

> Met us; they talk'd; I whispered, let'us goe,
> 'T may be you smell him not, truely I doe. . . .

Such anecdotal, conversational passages, breaking up an
originally orthodox metre, are the real stuff of satire:
and here Donne is using its technique with gusto. Again,
we need not suppose that, in writing such a passage as
the following:

> Why should's't thou (that dost not onely approve,
> But in ranke itchy lust, desire, and love
> The nakednesse and barenesse to enjoy,
> Of thy plumpe muddy whore or prostitute boy)
> Hate vertue, though shee be naked, and bare?

the future Dean of St. Paul's was not enjoying the conventional satirist's role and its attendant licence. Like
Lear's just gods, the satirist will gladly

> of our pleasant vices
> Make instruments to plague us

and will not write satire if he is afraid to go into detail
about the practices he has made it his business to casti-
gate. But Donne's condemnations of lawyers, suitors
and courtiers, though originally and forcefully expressed,
are yet conventionally derived.

It is illuminating to turn from Donne's satires to
those of another Elizabethan satirist, John Marston,[1]
who begins the proem to his third book of satires with
the clumsy, revealing pedantry of this couplet:

> In serious jest and jesting seriousness,
> I strive to scourge polluting beastlinesse.

Marston's crude, heavy moral *exempla* belong to a
literary style that seems, beside Donne's, antique as well
as antic:

[1] He was, within a few years, Donne's contemporary and like him took
Anglican orders later in his life.

O what dry braine melts not sharp mustard rhyme,
To purge the snottery of our slimy time!
Hence idle *cave*! Vengeance pricks me on
When mart is made of fair religion.
Reformed bald Trebus swore, in Romish quier,
He sold God's essence for a poor denier.
The Egyptians adored Osiris
To Garlick yielding all devotions.
O happy garlick, but thrice happy you
Whose senting gods in your large gardens grew. . . .

This is Juvenalian *saeva indignatio*, or a vernacular attempt thereat. The naïve Marstonian precept 'I hate no man but man's impietie' is the sort of moralization with which satire normally justified itself. In so far as Marston as a satirist approaches such greater poets as Juvenal or Swift, he becomes like them a fierce reactionary and, in the final analysis, an anti-humanist. (So Shakespeare's most satiric play is also his most reactionary and anti-humanistic, *Timon of Athens*.) Donne is one of the most humanistic of the great English poets, and therefore one of the least typical of satirists. The type of Marstonian polemic which the Church's ban on satire in 1599 sought to exterminate was not only alien to Donne's temperament as an artist but was also a weapon which a man who hoped to identify himself with the State would not wish to wield too publicly. But it must be added that those who saw copies of Donne's satires greatly admired them, and indeed they are amazingly mature, nimble, vigorous and effective—far more so than Marston's. Their vitality, and their author's huge gifts as a liberator of language, put them high in their class, and if Donne had left no other verse he would be an important late Elizabethan poet. In an early letter Donne told a friend, 'I am no great voyager in other men's works': and if we take this to be a reference to contemporary English, rather than continental, letters, there is reason to think he was not merely being youthfully arrogant. He had none of his friend Ben Jonson's lively and impressive interest in English literature, and his early verse has a curious, almost contemptuous originality, achieving as it does a remarkable revolution in the language as a poetical tool, but a private revolution in which he himself professed little critical interest. Donne put much more into satire than any English writer did before him, and in any history of English verse his satires would have to be described as a landmark.

4. VERSE-LETTERS

Something has already been said of two of Donne's most famous verse-letters, *The Storme* and *The Calme*: we know the occasion that prompted them and the praise they drew from Ben Jonson. In a way they are exceptional, for they were the product of personal experiences which must, even in less articulate men, have clamoured to be recorded. They are carefully elaborated, with an eloquence and strength that mark them out as among the best pieces of descriptive narrative in Elizabethan verse. Yet Donne's treatment of his adventures is characteristically ingenious and witty:

> Onely the Calenture[1] together drawes
> Deare friends, which meet dead in great fishes jawes;
> And on the hatches as on Altars lyes
> Each one, his owne Priest and owne Sacrifice.

The spirit is one of controlled but fantastic bravado. Donne is after all writing a letter to amuse his friend Brooke and, perhaps, to impress him with his adventure.

All Donne's verse-letters impress us, his eaves-dropping readers, with their author's unique personality.

[1] The tropical delirium which caused sailors to leap into the sea.

He was surely the most civilized as well as one of the
most learned of the poets of his day: but the great
qualities of his occasional verse are its[nimbleness and
variety, its charms and surprises, which are there because
the mind behind the verses is nimble, varied, charming
and capable of surprising by its alertness and originality.
Not that Donne is merely able to turn a graceful compliment to a great lady—

> Madame,
>   You have refin'd mee, and to worthyest things
> (Vertue, Art, Beauty, Fortune,) now I see
> Rarenesse, or use, not nature value brings;

—it is the intellectual use he makes of the compli-
ments (which the age required) that distinguishes them:

> For, as dark texts need notes: there[1] some must bee
> To usher vertue and say, *This is shee.*

Such a simile, scholarly yet witty, and presented with
genuine feeling, could only come from Donne. The
whole letter from which that couplet comes (it is
addressed to the Countess of Bedford) is full of such
evidence of interest in every branch of human activity.

Several of the best of the verse-letters are addressed
to the Countess of Bedford. They usually begin with a
gracefully turned compliment, respectful yet witty:
then Donne will go on to make the most and the best
of necessity by enlarging the compliment in widening
circles of imaginative wit which, while remaining
'concentrique unto' Lucy, also embrace topics of
general interest. The compliment to one woman becomes an observation on human nature as a whole.

> T' have written then, when you writ, seem'd to mee
> Worst of spirituall vices, Simony,

[1] i.e. at the Court.

And not t' have written then, seems little lesse
Then worst of civil vices, thanklessenesse.
In this, my debt I seem'd loath to confess,
In that, I seem'd to shunne beholdingnesse.
But 'tis not soe; *nothings*, as I am, may
Pay all they have, and yet have all to pay.
Such borrow in their payments, and owe more
By having leave to write so, then before.

After these charming nothings, Donne goes on to praise
Lucy for her virtue, uniquely preserved among court
corruptions:

I have beene told, that vertue in Courtiers hearts
Suffers an Ostracisme, and departs.
Profit, ease, fitnesse, plenty, bid it goe,
But whither, only knowing you, I know. . . .

She can never know her own worth, which modesty is
itself a good part of that worth.

But since to you, your praises discords bee,
Stoop others ills to meditate with mee.

And with that graceful lead and invitation, Donne can
embark on his real, self-proposed theme:

Oh! to confesse wee know not what we should,
Is halfe excuse: wee know not what we would:
Lightnesse depresseth us, emptinesse fills,
We sweat and faint, yet still goe downe the hills.

How true that is, and at once we have forgotten that
we are looking over Lucy's shoulder: this is the human
condition and we are looking, through Donne's eyes,
over humanity's shoulder. Unerringly, time and again,
Donne astonishes because he can write the poetry of
accomplishment so well and, at the same time, offer
worthwhile and original observations about human
character and behaviour: for example,

> Good seed degenerates, and oft obeyes
> The soyles disease, and into cockle strayes;
> Let the minds thoughts be but transplanted so,
> Into the body,'and bastardly they grow.
> What hate could hurt our bodies like our love?

That last line is a brilliant stroke, and the climax of a carefully organized passage: yet there it lies, buried away in a courtly, unread verse-letter, of which one must read fifty lines before one comes on it at all.

Another very beautiful poem addressed to Lucy, written not in couplets but in five-line stanzas, is one written on New Year's Day, 'this twilight of two yeares'. Its theme is, that Donne, in gratitude for having known Lucy, would perpetuate her virtues in verse. Yet, says the poet,

> . . . my verse built of your just praise, might want
> Reason and likelihood, the firmest Base,
> And made of miracle, now faith is scant,
> Will vanish soone, and so possesse no place. . . .

Therefore he will

> leave, lest truth be'endanger'd by my praise,
> And turne to God, who knowes I thinke this true.

That lovely line is the beginning of what Donne calls in the last line of the poem a 'private Ghospell'. And, with a simplicity that is too practical to be merely pious, Donne in the rest of this remarkable letter commends Lucy to the wisdom of God:

> Hee will best teach you, how you should lay out
> His stock of *beauty, learning, favour, blood*;
> He will perplex security with doubt,
> And cleare those doubts; hide from you'and shew
>   you good,
> And so increase your appetite and food;

There are five more verses, all as fine, of which one more
may be quoted:

> He will make you speake truths, and credibly,
> And make you doubt, that others doe not so:
> Hee will provide you keyes and locks, to spie,
> And scape spies, to good ends, and hee will shew
> What you may not acknowledge, what not know.

Such writing is rooted in an age which is still, for all
its modernity, an age of faith: God will 'perplex security
with doubt', but he will also 'clear those doubts'. It
is hard for us, in our age of brash anxieties and desperate
spiritual isolation, to estimate the beautiful propriety
of this poem, written to offer reasons for linking, not
isolating, human sympathies. In any case, Donne has
forestalled our objection to a poem we were not meant
to see: God, he says,

> useth oft, when such a heart mis-sayes,
> To make it good, for, such a praiser prayes.

Whoever praises virtue, whatever terms of reference
he chooses to employ, that man prays. This letter comes
unmistakably from the heart. When Donne turns a
compliment to a great lady, as in this extract from a
poem to the Countess of Huntingdon, he does not
merely flatter but, as he says himself, is 'Speaker of the
Universe' and so (but still without pompousness) a
witness, not to policy's opinion, but to the truth of
Virtue herself.

> And if I flatter any, 'tis not you
> But my owne judgment, who did long agoe
> Pronounce, that all these praises should be true,
> And vertue should your beauty,'and birth outgrow.
>
> Now that my prophesies are all fulfill'd,
> Rather then God should not be honour'd too,
> And all these gifts confess'd, which hee instill'd,
> Your selfe were bound to say that which I doe.

So I, but your Recorder am in this,
Or mouth, or Speaker of the universe,
A ministeriall Notary, for 'tis
Not I, but you and fame, that make this verse;

I was your Prophet in your younger dayes,
And now your Chaplain, God in you to praise.

I have already quoted (see page 25) a passage from the verse-letter to Sir Henry Wotton. This is one of the finest of Donne's pieces in this genre, and shows him at his closest to his great contemporary Jonson (compare the latter's poem to Sir Robert Wroth). Both poets modelled their verse-letters on the epistles and satires of Horace and Persius and the longer epigrams (really verse-letters) of Martial. These poets wrote in a relaxed, intimate, conversational style, and their so-called 'satires' (unlike most of Juvenal's) are largely reflective rather than aggressive, offering advice to the friend rather than abuse of the world.

5. EPITHALAMIONS

The first of Donne's three epithalamia or marriage-songs was written for the marriage of the Princess Elizabeth on St. Valentine's Day, 1613. In this poem Donne, says Grierson, comes in places near in style to Spenser, supreme master of the epithalamium. Decoration, a tapestry-like use of visual imagery, does certainly occur in the early stanzas: yet in the last two, Donne 'abstracts' the consummation he is supposed to be glorifying, in a characteristic, purely intellectual conceit:

> Here lyes a shee Sunne, and a hee Moone here,
>   She gives the best light to his Spheare,
>   Or each is both, and all, and so
> They unto one another nothing owe,
>   And yet they doe, but are
> So just and rich in that coyne which they pay,
> That neither would, nor needs forbeare, nor stay . . .
>
> . . . And by this act of these two Phenixes
>   Nature againe restored is.

Here Donne is no longer weaving a Spenserian carpet of sensual colours; instead of describing the ritual symbols of the marriage union, he thinks about its philosophical implications: the event as such is of little value in his scheme of thought, unless it can be related to his whole metaphysic.

The second epithalamium was written for the marriage of the Earl of Somerset, the King's favourite and chief minister, in December 1613.[1] It is introduced by an 'eclogue' in the style of Theocritus' and Virgil's dialogue-poems, in which two shepherds, usually masks with Greek names, discuss problems of the day. The form has been successfully revived in our own day by Mr. Louis MacNeice in his *Eclogue for Christmas*. Donne's two 'shepherds', Allophanes and Idios, discuss the marriage, which was of course the event of the season, and it is to be assumed that the second shepherd in this eclogue is meant to be the poet himself: 'Allophanes *finding* Idios *in the country in Christmas time, reprehends his absence from court at the marriage of the Earle of Somerset;* Idios *gives an account of his purpose therein and of his absence thence.*' Idios is the Greek word for a private citizen,

[1] See above, p. 42.

a man with no official position in the State. Now Idios in this eclogue makes two speeches. In his first he defends his absence from court on the ground that

> . . . reclus'd hermits often times do know
> More of heavens glory, then a worldling can

(not exactly a compliment to the occasion); while in arguing that, as man is the epitome of the world, and man's heart an epitome of creation, so is the country the epitome of court life (the two having 'sweet peace' in common), Donne is surely being ironic. Then Allophanes (who is probably Sir Robert Ker, a friend of Donne and a protégé of Somerset, with whom he shared the common surname of Ker: hence Allophanes as 'other seemer', the Greek meaning of the coined name, with perhaps a deliberate hint of 'dissembler') makes a long vague speech barely mentioning Somerset, but praising the King and his court, unique in history, where

> men need whisper nothing, and yet may;

(which is clever both as flattery and as verse). To this Idios answers that he knew it all and

> onely therefore I withdrew.
> To know and feele all this, and not to have
> Words to expresse it, makes a man a grave
> Of his owne thoughts; I would not therefore stay
> At a great feast, having no Grace to say.

Idios here appears to doubt his ability to express the correct sentiments: the word 'grace' seems, too, to hint that (as a man soon to take holy orders) he has no benediction to add to an occasion he secretly dislikes. Again, at the end of his speech he refers to the nuptial song which follows the eclogue as testifying that

> I did unto that day some sacrifice.

—burnt offering? and also sacrifice of scruple in having addressed himself to a political racketeer? At any rate, after the epithalamium proper (a sequence of elaborate stanzas) there is the following little epilogue:

Idios:

> As I have brought this song, that I may doe
> A perfect sacrifice, I'll burne it too.

(Donne expresses a desire to destroy the poem.)

Allophanes:

> No sir. This paper I have justly got,
> . . . the perfume is not
> His only that presents it, but of all. . . .
> Nor may your selfe be Priest: But let me goe,
> Backe to the Court, and I will lay 't upon
> Such Altars as prize your devotion.

There is self-defensive irony here, as if Ker were made to tell Donne: 'You may as well try and do yourself a bit of good.'

The third epithalamium is much earlier than the other two, being 'made at Lincolns Inn', presumably in the 1590's when Donne was a student there. It can perhaps more truly be described as Spenserian than can Princess Elizabeth's epithalamium: of the few touches which are un-Spenserian and truly Donnian, 'like to a grave', at the beginning of line 5 of stanza 1, is the most typical: it is an intrusion which would be unthinkable in a truly Spenserian marriage-song.

6. THE PROGRESSE OF THE SOULE

This curious poem was written in 1601. Ben Jonson refers to it as 'the conceit of Dones Transformation or Μετεμψύχωσις' and says of it that Donne 'never wrote but one sheet and now, since he was made doctor, repenteth highly and seeketh to destroy all his poems'. The words 'first song' appear at the beginning of the poem, and it is clear from the seventh stanza that Donne intended to conclude his 'poema satyricon', as he calls it, by showing that the 'soul' which began life in Eve's apple had turned up again in Queen Elizabeth, the arch-heretic and descendant of Cain's wife. He does not reach this conclusion, however, and the last verse may be a hastily contrived ending to an idea of which Donne (whose Catholic sympathies, by 1601, were weakening) had grown tired.

The poem is one of which Dr. Donne would have had ample reason to repent (it is indecent as well as un-patriotic). He used the title again, perhaps by way of expiation, for his second 'Anniversary' written eleven years later, in which he followed, with Christian fervour, the soul of a dead girl on its direct, innocent and ortho-dox flight to Paradise. But in the 'conceit of his Trans-formation' the soul makes a very different sort of progress. Beginning in the apple on the 'forbidden learned tree', it passes, 'bent on gallant mischief,' into a succession of creatures—mandrake, sparrow, fish, mouse, elephant, wolf and ape—until the ape tries to seduce a woman when the soul takes refuge in her. And there (apart from the tagged-on last verse) the poem abruptly ends. Perhaps it is the last work of Jack Donne's carefree days, before marriage, responsi-bility and anxiety brought him from the aesthetic to the ethical plane of existence. At any rate, it is his most fantastic piece of speculation (with its mock-serious Latin inscription 'sacred to infinity') and provides evi-dence of a youthful interest (which many passages in his later works show he never completely lost) in the Kabbala: that eccentric Jewish theosophical system, in which Pythagorean metempsychosis finds a place, had a considerable influence on Catholic Renaissance thinkers like Pico della Mirandola (whom Donne certainly read), particularly in respect of its view of the macrocosm and of man as the epitome, the microcosm, and of its preoccupation with natural science. The descriptions of the various creatures in *The Progresse of the Soule* are witty examples of humanistic curiosity about natural history:

> Is any kinde subject to rape like fish?
> Ill unto man, they neither doe, nor wish:
> Fishers they kill not, nor with noise awake,
> They doe not hunt, nor strive to make a prey
> Of beasts. . . .
> > (Stanza xxix)

> Natures great master-peece, an Elephant,
> The onely harmlesse great thing; the giant
> Of beasts, who thought, no more had gone, to make
> > one wise
> But to be just, and thankfull, loth to offend,
> (Yet nature hath given him no knees to bend)
> Himselfe he up-props, on himselfe relies,
> And foe to none, suspects no enemies,
> Still sleeping stood; vex't not his fantasie
> Blacke dreames; like an unbent bow, carelesly
> His sinewy Proboscis did remisly lie.
> > (Stanza xxxix)

This liveliness and technical adroitness hold, I think, our interest in a *tour de force* which, as Donne tells the reader in the last verse, 'just so much courts thee, as thou dost it', although perhaps the courting of so lengthy a conceit upon so arcane a theme is nowadays an acquired taste. But even if the poem as a whole is dismissed as a young intellectual's unfinished would-be masterpiece, a kind of enormous joke, three interesting personal stanzas in it, rather different from the rest, should be mentioned. They are stanzas iv–vi, addressed

by Donne to 'Destiny, the Commissary of God', with
a request to be told how much longer he has to live.
'I am thirty now,' he says, using the very Ovidian peri-
phrasis 'six lustres', 'and unless I am guaranteed another
thirty years I had much better

> save
> Th' expense of brain and spirit; that my grave
> His right and due, a whole unwasted man may have.

'But if I get a good long innings,' he continues, 'I will
battle cheerfully through my present existence':

> For though through many streights, and lands I roame,
> I launch at paradise, and I saile towards home.

As the rest of the stanza shows, Donne is here typically
relating his bizarre theme to himself. The soul of heresy
began in Paradise (in the apple), roamed through such
'prisons of flesh' as Luther and Mahomet, and is now
at rest in England in Elizabeth. The poet's soul, too
(does Donne hint that he is himself something, already,
of a heretic?), 'cometh from afar' and is now at rest
in England but is aiming, in accordance with Pythagorean teaching, at a completion of its cycle by a return
to the place whence it came, a return home. But the
line 'I launch at paradise, and I saile towards home' is a
moving one, and cannot help carrying echoes of orthodox medieval *contemptus mundi* which it does not strictly
require. Similarly, stanza viii contains some fine straight-
forward lines about Christ, three of which Donne was
to use again in a strictly Christian context in his cycle
of sacred sonnets called *La Corona*.

7. EPICEDES AND OBSEQUIES

There are (excluding the 'Anniversaries') seven of
these elegies celebrating the deaths of notable con-

temporaries: most of them are products of Donne's middle years. The longest and most ambitious of them is the *Obsequies to the Lord Harrington*[1] which may be taken as representative. One of the few passages from Donne quoted at length by Dr. Johnson, in his attack on the metaphysicals (in his *Life* of Cowley), is taken from this poem: Johnson means to show how a metaphysical poet, confronted with the theme of 'night', will 'look out not for images but conceits':

> Thou seest mee here at midnight, now all rest;
> Times dead-low water; when all minds devest
> To morrows businesse, when the labourers have
> Such rest in bed, that their last Church-yard grave,
> Subject to change, will scarce be'a type of this,
> Now when the clyent, whose last hearing is
> To morrow, sleeps, when the condemned man,
> (Who when he opes his eyes, must shut them than
> Againe by death,) although sad watch hee keepe,
> Doth practice dying by a little sleepe,
> Thou at this midnight seest me. . . .

It is a pity that Johnson could not acknowledge the qualities of this impressive passage. Apart from the fine pathos and irony of 'doth practice dying by a little sleepe', the whole description is full of firm strokes, delineated in Donne's strictest manner. Possibly Johnson, with his deep dread of the hereafter, disliked what to Donne was an essential analogy and connexion between sleep and death.

The whole elegy follows the usual formal pattern of lamenting the untimely death of a valuable man:

> Now I grow sure, that if a man would have
> Good companie, his entry is a grave.

[1] John Harington, 2nd Baron Exton, brother of Lucy Countess of Bedford. He died, aged twenty-one, in 1614.

I

The idea that Harington was

> forc'd to bee
> For lack of time, his owne epitome

is worked out with great care in a logical series of metaphysical analogies. To illustrate the thesis that 'in good short lives virtues are faine to thrust/And to be sure betimes to get a place', Donne draws analogies from the quick flight of an angel, and thence from the speed of a perfect reader who

> doth not dwell,
> On every syllable, nor stay to spell,
> Yet without doubt, hee doth distinctly see
> And lay together every A, and B;

Then the dead man's soul is likened to a circle whose ends of birth and death have closed up over-quickly; thence to a compass (a favourite image of Donne's) of which one foot was fixed in heaven and the other might have ranged 'In the most large extent through every path/Which the whole world, or man the abridgement hath'. The next image is a complicated geographical one, the idea being that all lives are circles but can be of various sizes, as the polar circles are smaller than the equatorial yet all perfect and complete. From the circle or cycle of Harington's soul we may learn, says Donne, 'both how to live well young and how to die', but *not* how to grow old nobly. Yet just as we need an example for the former, so we do for the latter: and Harington is mock-reproached for not providing it. More of us grow old than die young: the more need therefore for guidance. The next image is of the good life as a clock by which we can regulate our own lives. 'Small pocket clocks' are unreliable and private, but great clocks 'placed to inform whole towns' do more harm to more people if they are wrong ('small clocks' faults only on the wearer fall'). Why then did not Harington, taking his time from the Sun (God), so true was his soul, stay alive longer to be our guide?

So after these 'modern' images Donne reaches his respectful conclusion:

> So, though, triumphant soule, I dare to write,
> Mov'd with a reverentiall ánger, thus,
> That thou so earely wouldst abandon us;
> Yet I am farre from daring to dispute
> With that great soveraigntie, whose absolute
> Prerogative hath thus dispens'd with thee. . . .

This poem and the other funeral elegies are good working examples of how the resources of the metaphysical technique enable the poet, who probably feels no personal grief, to offer a variety of comfort, appropriate yet original, upon the formal occasion of death: the conceits and analogies are as carefully chosen as acquaintances would nowadays choose flowers for the wreath. Donne begins another elegy—upon the death of a lady, probably Mistress Bulstrode—with the more familiar words of feigned inarticulateness:

> Language thou art too narrow, and too weake
> To ease us now; great sorrow cannot speake;

Perhaps it cannot; but the patron had a literary man to speak for him: 'Knew'st thou some would, that knew her not, lament?'

8. ANNIVERSARIES

In 1610 Elizabeth, daughter of Donne's friend and patron Sir Robert Drury, died at the age of fifteen. In the two subsequent years Donne commemorated her death with two very long and elaborate funeral elegies.[1]

[1] See above, p. 31.

The idea behind them is that the death of one so young and innocent leaves the world empty, rotten and virtueless. Using all his knowledge of scholastic doctrine, Donne concentrates into these transitional poems all the disillusion with this life and hope of the next with which his mind had been filled during the difficult and frustrating decade that preceded his decision to prepare himself for the Church. At times his thought crystallizes into a felt intensity of passion that leaves the original cause and subject of the poems far behind. The poems were severely criticized for their extravagance, yet the ideas which Donne pursues in them are frequently realized in magnificent passages of verse.

In the first poem, *The Anatomie of the World*, Donne apostrophizes—and attacks—our 'sick world':

> Her death hath taught us dearely, that thou art
> Corrupt and mortall in thy purest part.
> Let no man say, the world it selfe being dead,
> 'Tis labour lost to have discovered
> The worlds infirmities, since there is none
> Alive to study this dissection:
> For there's a kinde of World remaining still
> Though shee which did inanimate and fill
> The world, be gone, yet in this last long night,
> Her Ghost doth walke; that is, a glimmering light,
> A faint weake love of vertue, and of good,
> Reflects from her. . . .

The various arguments of the poem cannot be analysed here, but the key passage is the celebrated one beginning 'And new Philosophy calls all in doubt' which so well sums up that peculiarly Jacobean *weltschmerz*, with its sense of decay, certainties and values vanishing, the inadequacy of the new learning, and its emphasis on sickness and corruption spreading like a contagious disease, with man as the carrier, through the world.

Donne has caught perfectly the spirit of his time, which saw the world through Hamlet's eyes. But the Christian could remember that corruption was only of the body, that prison of the soul. Death, then, is the true birth and the only release from infection into the pure life of immortality:

> for though the soule of man
> Be got when man is made, 'tis borne but than
> When man doth die; our body's as the wombe,
> And, as a Mid-wife, death directs it home.

We are moving further towards Donne's religious verse.

In the *Second Anniversary* (*The Progresse of the Soule*) we move still closer. From the disorders of this world Donne follows the departed soul into the perfection of the next. Meanwhile we who are left behind must 'forget this rotten world': it is 'fragmentary rubbidge'. In lines 85–120, a great meditation beginning 'Thinke then, my soule, that death is but a Groome' depicts the dying man who ought to rejoice because it is his weeping friends, who seem whole, who are really sick, and himself who is about to be cured for ever of the sickness of life. Another fine passage beginning 'But thinke that Death hath now enfranchis'd thee' likens the soul leaving the body at death to a bullet discharged from a rusty pistol. Throughout, death is shown as a release, a return home.

The next part of the *Second Anniversary* is devoted to a less passionate and very detailed series of arguments to show how little a thing life is, how little we know of ourselves, how we were born, or how it is that we are immortal souls: even

> Why grasse is greene, or why our blood is red,
> Are mysteries which none have reach'd unto.

We are the slaves of 'sense' (i.e. our five senses: slaves to, because implicit believers in, the reliability of

Plato's 'phenomenal world') and 'fantasy' (i.e. imagination): 'small things seem great below'

> . . . But up unto the watch-towre get,
> And see all things despoyl'd of fallacies:
> Thou shalt not peep through lattices of eyes
> Nor heare through Labyrinths of eares, nor learne
> By circuit or collections to discerne.
> In heaven thou straight know'st all. . . .

This is the idealist's *contemptus mundi*, belittling earthly knowledge as 'an hundred controversies of an ant'. All earthly things change, deceive and die, all earthly joys are accidental while heaven's alone are 'essential'. So we enter the last section of the poem, a long reasoned rhapsody on the bliss of the resurrected soul as the bride of Christ.

> Up, up, my drowsie Soule, where thy new eare
> Shall in the Angels songs no discord heare;
> Where thou shalt see the blessed Mother-maid
> Joy in not being that, which men have said.
> Where she is exalted more for being good
> Then for her interest of Mother-hood. . . .

So the song, too, mounts with the ardent soul

> Up to those Martyrs, who did calmly bleed
> Oyle to th' Apostles Lamps, dew to their seed . . .

and the transition from the secular to the divine poems is complete. 'Earth had attained to heaven, there was no more near nor far.'

DIVINE POEMS

I. LA CORONA

'CORONA', in Donne's favourite language, Spanish, can mean seven decades of the rosary offered to the Virgin. *La Corona* is a set of seven linked sonnets sent, with a separate dedicatory sonnet, to Lady Herbert in 1607 (the accompanying sonnet links her with St. Mary Magdalen through their common name of Magdalen). In the first sonnet Donne speaks of having composed the work in 'low devout melancholy'. The remaining six sonnets are meditations on six of the fifteen Mysteries of the rosary: the first three are 'Joyful Mysteries', the Annunciation, Nativity and [Finding in the] Temple; the fourth is a 'Sorrowful Mystery', the Crucifixion, and the last two 'Glorious Mysteries', the Resurrection and the Ascension.

The poems were written during Donne's most obscure and frustrated years, shortly before *Biathanatos* (the prose treatise in which he argues that suicide, under certain circumstances, is justifiable), and are, I think, an attempt to find in a religious exercise some respite from an unsatisfactory and depressing everyday existence: that is, they were prompted more by a deep interest in theology than by that personal need for, and effort towards, salvation which characterizes the more celebrated *Holy Sonnets*. Such a heartfelt reference to death as this:

> For, at our end begins our endlesse rest;
> The first last end, now zealously possest,
> With a strong sober thirst, my soule attends.
>
> (*La Corona*, Sonnet 1)

suggests Donne felt the need of a steady, formal religious discipline as a cure for melancholy, the need to 'forget this rotten world' rather than to accept it through Christ.

The six meditations are less personal, then, than most of the *Holy Sonnets*. They are formal compositions on the great traditional devotional themes, resembling some noble series of full-page miniatures of the Life of Christ at the beginning of a medieval psalter. Each sonnet starts with a text-line, which is the same as the last line of the preceding sonnet, while the last line of sonnet 7 is the same as the first line of sonnet 1: thus the cycle is, as Donne says, 'woven together'. This formal pattern is the poetic correlative of a theology itself still formal rather than personal. It is perhaps worth recalling that three fine lines in the second sonnet (Annunciation) were first written in 1601—they occur in the satirical fantasy *The Progresse of the Soule*.

Yet this is not to say that a personal attempt to respond artistically to the truths of Christianity is not made anywhere in *La Corona*. It is. In the first four sonnets, these truths are deeply felt, if not passionately applied. But No. 5 (Crucifying) ends on a more insistent note, a note of private prayer:

> Now thou art lifted up, draw me to thee,
> And at thy death giving such liberall dole,
> *Moyst, with one drop of thy blood, my dry soule.*

One is reminded of an earlier cry, a cry of intenser and more imperious agony:

> See see where Christ's blood streams in the firmament!
> One drop would save my soul, half a drop.

And in the seventh and final sonnet we get a genuine foretaste of that private devotional intensity which illuminates the *Holy Sonnets*:

> O strong Ramme, which hast batter'd heaven for mee,
> Mild Lambe, which with thy blood, hast mark'd the path;
> Bright Torch, which shin'st, that I the way may see,
> Oh, with thy owne blood quench thy owne just wrath. . . .

2. HOLY SONNETS

Donne wrote nineteen sacred sonnets beside the *La Corona* cycle, and it is to these that the general term *Holy Sonnets* usually refers. The last three of these sonnets, including one (No. XVII) which, by its reference to the death of the poet's wife, must belong to or after 1617, exist only in a single manuscript and were first printed by Gosse in 1894. Of the other sixteen, which exist in a number of manuscripts, twelve were first printed in the 1633 edition of Donne's poems, the other four in the 1635 edition. The problem of when the various sonnets were written is a complex, largely theological one,[1] but it seems likely that many of them belong to that period of doubt and intense thinking about his religion which preceded Donne's entry into the Church. A few of the poems indeed, by their occasional roughness of metre and phraseology, seem almost as if they were written before *La Corona*: but the years 1609–17 are probably the likeliest for the majority.

We know that during his years at Mitcham Donne was a prey to what he afterwards regarded with horror as the sin of melancholy—at times, the sin of despair. At that time, too, he was in poor physical health, and indeed, in 1608, seriously ill. It is to that illness of Jack Donne

---

[1] See Helen Gardner, *John Donne, The Divine Poems*, 1953.

that those sonnets which speak as if death were imminent, probably refer, rather than to the much later illness (1623) of the *Devotions*. Three sonnets come in here: No. I,[1] 'Thou hast made me, and shall thy work decay?', No. IV, 'O my black soule', and No. VI, 'This is my playes last scene'. In each of these Donne speaks as if not merely 'his soules sickness which is sin', but also a dire bodily sickness, was affecting him:

> Repaire me now, for now mine end doth haste,
> I runne to death, and death meets me as fast,
> And all my pleasures are like yesterday; (I)

> Oh my black Soule! now thou art summoned
> By sicknesse, deaths herald, and champion; (IV)

> And gluttonous death, will instantly unjoynt
> My body, and soule . . . (VI)

In these rather sombre sonnets, the poet seeks strength, grace and forgiveness from Christ, who is asked to rescue him from the toils of sin. . . . 'And thou like Adamant draw mine iron heart', and again, 'Except Thou rise and for thine owne worke fight'. This struggle to leave 'the World, the Fleshe, the Devill' (the phrase occurs twice in the *Holy Sonnets*) is the theme of two more sonnets, II and XIV. These sonnets do not suggest physical sickness, but a desire for resignation to God— though again arguing passionately that the author is himself powerless to escape from Satan without active aid. No. II, 'As due by many titles I resign', states that the poet is God's rightful possession which Satan is trying to take from God. God is asked to take back his creature by force. The line

> And Satan hates mee, yet is loth to lose mee

---

[1] The sonnets are here numbered as in Grierson's edition.

suggests Donne's feeling, during the last years of his secular life, that all the world is against him and has rejected him, but that despite this rejection he cannot yet manage wholly to surrender to God of his own will. Lines 12 and 13 too,

> Oh I shall soone despaire, when I doe see
> That thou lov'st mankind well, yet wilt'not chuse mee,

though general in meaning, seem specially applicable to the pre-ordination years. In this sonnet Christ appears as the sought-for lover and Donne as a temple usurped by the Devil. Sonnet XIV, the splendid 'Batter my heart, three person'd God', uses the same idea and imagery more passionately. Again the image of usurpation occurs:

> I, like an usurpt towne, to'another due,
> Labour to'admit you, but Oh, to no end.

And not merely the recurrence of 'due' (which comes in line 1 of No. II) but, more significantly, the recurrence of the word 'ravish', helps us to see both these sonnets as expressions of a regretted thraldom to Satan: in both Christ is beseeched to take full possession, as victor-lover, of the poet's soul.

'Why doth he [Satan] steale, nay ravish that's[1] thy right?' asks Donne in sonnet II, and in the famous ending of No. XIV he cries

> for I,
> Except you'enthrall mee, never shall be free,
> Nor ever chast, except you ravish mee.

Throughout the *Holy Sonnets* runs Donne's demand for God to become active in his own life. Thus he sees his need for God in terms of that life and describes it in those terms—in the last quotation the idea of God as the

---

[1] i.e. that which is.

lover whose love alone is chastity is a profoundly central image. With the contemporary language of profane love, Donne is able to realize the traditional idea of divine love as a concrete and important experience, in the communication of which he is unequalled by any other English poet.

So, again, in the 1617 sonnet on his wife's death (No. XVII) Donne imputes to God 'tender jealousy' of world, flesh and devil as His rivals for possession of his soul. He has left a most interesting and illuminating defence of this practice of putting secular passions to divine use, in a sermon preached in 1617: 'That soul that hath been transported upon any particular worldly pleasure, when it is entirely turned upon God, and the contemplation of his all-sufficiency and abundance, doth find in God fit subject and just occasion, to exercise that same affection piously and religiously, which had before so sinfully transported and possessed it.' And in the same sermon he says: 'So will a voluptuous man who is turned to God find plenty and deliciousness enough in him to feed his soul . . . and so an angry and passionate man will find zeal enough in the house of God to eat him up'; that final quotation from Psalm 69 is also used at the end of the fifth holy sonnet. Another passage adduces the authority of the religious-erotic literary tradition derived from the Song of Songs: 'Solomon whose disposition was amorous and excessive in the love of women, when he turned to God he departed not utterly from his old phrase and language, but having put a new and a spiritual tincture and form and habit in all his thoughts and words, he conveys all his loving approaches and applications to God, and all Gods gracious answers to his amorous soul into songs and Epithalamions and . . . marriages between God and his Church and between God and his soul.' Once more we get the echo of language used in the *Holy Sonnets*, 'and let *mine amorous soule* court thy mild dove' (sonnet XVIII).

We know from the seventeenth holy sonnet on the death of his wife, 'Since she whom I lov'd hath payd her last debt', that Donne later dated the awakening of his religious feelings to the beginning of the new century—

> the admyring her my mind did whett
> To seeke thee God;

so that a few of the more doctrinal, less intense, sonnets *could* have been written before *La Corona*, though the manuscript groupings do not single out these sonnets from the more obviously 'middle-period' ones. Sonnets IX and XII, on the difference between man and the rest of creation in respect of the former's power to sin, are rather preoccupied with theological problems, but are not without their personal point of return—particularly No. IX, with its tearful expostulation

> O God? Oh! of thine onely worthy blood,
> And my teares, make a heavenly Lethean flood. . . .

a passage which is, however, surpassed by the beautiful fifth sonnet, full of Renaissance *wanderlust*:

> You which beyond that heaven which was most high
> Have found new sphears, and of new lands can write,
> Powre new seas in mine eyes, that so I might
> Drowne my world with my weeping earnestly,
> Or wash it, if it must be drown'd no more.

One is here almost back in the world of tears in which so many of Donne's more poignant secular poems swim —tears standing for regret and for regretted melancholy as in sonnet III:

> O might those sighes and teares returne againe
> Into my breast and eyes, which I have spent,
> That I might in this holy discontent
> Mourne with some fruit, as I have mourn'd in vaine;

'In mine idolatry', says the poet, referring to his profane days, 'I lavished tears on idle regret, and melancholy—a false grief for unworthy objects. Now this recollection grieves me and I see that tears wasted on sinful things were themselves a sin.' And sonnet III ends

> for, long, yet vehement griefe hath beene
> Th' effect and cause, the punishment and sinne.

(i.e. 'for a long time now, I have regretted—and still regret—my past which was itself full of false regret'). The phrase 'in my idolatry' comes again in sonnet XIII, which contains a reference to the poet's profane mistresses. This is the startling and beautiful 'What if this present were the world's last night?' in which he asks his soul

> Whether that countenance can thee affright,
> Teares in his eyes quench the amasing light. . . .

'If Christ appeared to me now, would he send me to hell? No, for surely his beauty is a sign that he will be merciful, an argument I used to use to women.' Beautiful women have been kind to me, so will not Christ also be kind?—such an analogy could have come, in such a context, from no one but Donne.

Donne's greatness as a religious poet lies in his truthfulness, in his having left in his *Holy Sonnets* a personal record of a brilliant mind struggling towards God. The goal is never in doubt. 'Truth stands', but it has to be won. It is the pilgrim's progress which we want to read. To a clever man who also believes in God, the task of responding adequately to divine grace and truth

is presumably the greatest task he can ever attempt.
But the intellectual greatness of the task is only part of
the story. Most religious experience is an emotional
awareness of inadequacy, fear, regret, self-contempt,
a constant fresh striving towards a God who does not
come uncalled. 'For us there is only the trying.' Only
for the few, saints, martyrs, mystics, does religious
experience mean only—or chiefly—triumph. St. John
of the Cross, St. Theresa, have written such verse. But
Donne's is not like theirs, though it has some of their
splendour. Donne is passionate but not transcendental.
He is eloquent, but with a subjective precision. He is
not afraid to analyse the appalling difficulties of faith:

> . . . when I would not
> I change in vowes, and in devotione.
> . . . I durst not view heaven yesterday; and to day
> In prayers and flattering speaches I court God:
> To morrow I quake with true feare of his rod.
> So my devout fitts come and go away
> Like a fantastique Ague: save that here
> Those are my best dayes, when I shake with feare.

Again, by means of the metaphysical paradox of the
sinner's 'best', i.e. healthiest, days being like a sick
man's worst days, Donne is able to put down, exactly
and memorably, the vacillations of the imperfect,
temperamental man. And throughout the *Holy Sonnets*
even for the 'black soul', trapped like a terrified criminal
in a dark alley between despair and death, the love of
God is felt as eternally available to effect a rescue. But
this love, just like the love of profane mistresses, must
be sought out, must be courted—not with 'flattering
speeches' but with all the humility and self-surrender
which the seeker can summon. What has been promised
to all must nevertheless be claimed individually by each.
'For as in Adam all have sinned, and must die, so in

Christ all shall be saved'; and Donne took for his emblem, Walton tells us, Christ affixed 'not to a cross but to an anchor (the emblem of hope)'. So, too, in his most famous hymn,[1] he invokes, as an anchor against his own dread of extinction, Christ's promise to a repentant mankind:

> I have a sinne of feare, that when I have spunne
> My last thred, I shall perish on the shore;
> But sweare by thy selfe, that at my death thy sonne[2]
> Shall shine as he shines now, and heretofore;
> And having done that, Thou hast done,[2]
> I feare no more.

We see here, with startling clearness, into Donne's mind. Intellectually, he has long accepted the presence of Christ in history and the truth of the New Testament. But he was no innocent, and in his most intimate religious poems he records how hard he had to fight against the sins of doubt and fear.

Donne thus attaches importance not only to the dogmatic aspects of Christianity but also to its psychotherapeutic qualities. He needed for himself that wholeness of mind and peace of heart which he knew could only come from a personal assimilation of the meaning of his religion. Such an attitude is characteristic of his whole mental outlook, his profound sympathy with the dark side of existence, his understanding of human weaknesses and desires. Intellectually, artistically, he vividly accepts the idealistic splendour of the Catholic world-picture. But as a man of the late Renaissance, living at a time when no theory, however perfect and unblemished, could protect him from a blemished and imperfect world, he had learnt also to see Christianity as a psycho-analytical prescription, a guide, not so much to conduct

---

[1] See above, p. 46.
[2] There is a pun on the poet's name, and, of course, on sun and son.

like Victorian Christianity, but to one's own thought-
processes. He had to see Christianity, in fact, as a double
force—as a doctrine and as a technique for believing
in that doctrine. And this technique is something a
man must master for himself 'here on this lowly
ground'.

The reaction of the individual to the enormous
symbols of Catholic truth is naturally often a sense of
terrified inadequacy. In the seventh holy sonnet:

> At the round earths imagined corners, blow
> Your trumpets, Angells, and arise, arise
> From death, you numberlesse infinities
> Of soules . . .

the octet transports our imagination to the traditional
scene of the Last Day, which is depicted as in some *Quat-
trocento* panel or fresco: the picture is crowded with
'numberlesse infinities of soules' going to their 'scattred
bodies'. But the poet himself is not part of this scene
and, in quiet contrast, the sestet is a prayer that what
has just been depicted shall not take place until he has
learnt how to repent:

> But let them sleepe, Lord, and mee mourne a space,
> For, if above all these, my sinnes abound,
> 'Tis late to aske abundance of thy grace,
> When wee are there . . .

This sonnet is a fine example of Donne's way of using
his traditional medieval material. As a preacher, he
affirmed that 'God at the general judgement shall never
reverse any particular judgement formerly given' and,
speaking of the sinner who dies repentant, described how
God would 'whisper gently to his departing soul' and
would 'drown and overcome with this soft music of his
all the clangour of the Angels trumpets'. Those things

K

he knew, professionally, and taught as a preacher: but as a poet he reveals the struggle he himself had to learn them: 'Teach mee how to repent.'

Donne's imagination was much exercised by this problem of the supreme challenger, death, whom he called, in a sermon preached in 1621, 'the last and in that respect the worst enemy'. In that sermon, as so often, he lingers a little upon the strength of that enemy, an enemy whom he seems almost to feel, with an intense and typical sense of drama, as fully worthy of its ultimate and sole conqueror: 'Death shall triumph over me God knows how many generations, till I shall be no more, till that Angel come, Who shall say, and swear, that time shall be no more.'

In the *Holy Sonnets*, the most uncompromising proclamation of the ultimate defeat of death is that of No. X, 'Death be not proud', though not until the last two lines is the Christian triumph specifically stated. Paradoxically, death is first called the slave, not of the angel of the resurrection, but of its own various modes or agents—Fate, chance, kings, and desperate men; while the idea of death being more pleasant than sleep because sleep is a mere counterpart of the real thing is really a metaphysical conceit. But in these sonnets Donne is not speaking professionally or doctrinally but is meditating privately upon that 'little world made cunningly of elements', the human soul, which, by God's will and grace, shall not be suffered to see corruption. Against his sense of sin and corruption, his regrets and his fears, Donne had to place in the balance all his faith in the New Testament—'Oh let this last Will stand!'—and in the salvation which has been promised to those who can learn to repent—as they must learn: once again Donne stresses the positive effort, the active struggle which each man must make.

One more sonnet should be mentioned: the very beautiful No. XVIII, 'Show me, deare Christ, thy spouse, so bright and clear', which is a personal prayer to Christ to let him see the true Church, undivided because indivisible. This is one of the three holy sonnets which remained uncopied and unprinted until Gosse found them at the end of the nineteenth century. It shows clearly that in his heart the ideal, universal Church meant more to Donne than any particular form of Christianity. It is the third satire over again, but what was there set forth with cheerful, debating-society reasonableness as a series of cogent and interesting arguments is now, rather desperately, felt as something which, like a vision, cannot be argued about, but only prayed for. In the satire Donne was not emotionally involved in the problem; it did not seem urgent:

> Seeke true religion. O where? Mirreus
> Thinking her unhous'd here, and fled from us,
> Seekes her at Rome, there, because hee doth know
> That shee was there a thousand yeares agoe.

But in the holy sonnet the strength of Donne's feeling is expressed in the surging stresses of a passionate plea to Christ himself, a plea for perfection and wholeness:

> Show me, deare Christ, thy spouse, so bright and clear.
> . . . Doth she, and did she, and shall she evermore
> On one, on seaven, or on no hill appeare?

England, Rome and Geneva are no longer presented as morality-figures, each with its own justification: it is no longer enough to keep the truth one has found. These local habitations and names become fused in the one figure, whose femininity is characteristically insisted on in the paradoxical conclusion of the sonnet. At last, in the bride of Christ, Donne rejoices in one—or in the idea of one?—who

> is most trew and pleasing to thee, then
> When she'is embraced and open to most men.

The bride of Christ is the mistress of the whole world.

3. MISCELLANEOUS DIVINE POEMS

Beside the *Holy Sonnets*, and the well-known *Hymn to God the Father* (which is No. 515 in the *English Hymnal*), Donne during the latter part of his life, says Walton, 'did also shorten and beguile many sad hours by composing other sacred ditties'. Among these is the hymn 'to God, my God, in my sicknesse', written, according to Walton, eight days before his death, though in Sir Julius Caesar's manuscript copy of it, now in the British Museum,[1] it is dated December 1623, Caesar evidently believing the sickness to have been that which produced the *Devotions*. This hymn is remarkable for its wholesale use of characteristically Donnian imagery drawn from the familiar Elizabethan *mappa mundi*. Discovery and far countries were to the Elizabethans vivid contemporary adventures and apt images to mirror the sense of discovery in the Elizabethan creative mind. The central image of the hymn is of the soul as a 'flat map': verses 2 and 3 introduce this image:

> Whilst my Physitians by their love are growne
> Cosmographers, and I their Mapp, who lie
> Flat on this bed, that by them may be showne
> That this is my South-west discoverie
> *Per fretum febris*, by these streights to die,

[1] Add. MS. 34324.

> I joy, that in these straits I see my West,
> For, though their currants yeeld returne to none,
> What shall my West hurt me? As West and East
> In all flatt Maps (and I am one) are one,
> So death doth touch the Resurrection.

The explanation of these last lines is given by Donne himself in one of his sermons:

> In a flat map, there goes no more to make West East, though they be distant in an extremity, but to paste that flat map upon a round body, and then West and East are all one.

The idea of straits, as paths to new lands which, save by these paths, are inaccessible (this idea occurs in verse 3), is also referred to in a sermon: 'a narrower way but to a better land'. So, in the hymn, the Anyan straits are the Behring straits (leading to the 'Easterne riches'), Magellan's straits lead to the Pacific, Gibraltar is the route for Jerusalem:

> All streights, and none but streights, are wayes to them.

The idea of west and east as one was natural to an Elizabethan, fascinated with the 'round world' as an exciting potent idea: when transferred to religion it is a paradox of central importance. The west is death, decline, the setting sun. But the same sun also rises, and Christ is named 'Oriens', which means both 'East' and 'Rising'. 'He looks upon him whose name is Rising' is the last sentence of Donne's epitaph, and in the religious poem written in couplets, dated Good Friday, 1613, *Riding Westward*, the same idea gets eloquent expression as technical geography widens into spiritual cosmography. The soul is not here a flat map, but a sphere. The body rides west, but the 'soul's form bends towards the East', i.e. towards Christ:

> There I should see a Sunne, by rising set,
> And by that setting endlesse day beget;
> But that Christ on this Crosse, did rise and fall,
> Sinne had eternally benighted all.
> Yet dare I'almost be glad, I do not see
> That spectacle of too much weight for mee.
> Who sees Gods face, that is selfe life,[1] must dye;
> What a death were it then to see God dye?

This use of paradox was perfectly natural to Donne, and is easy enough—perhaps too easy—for us to take. Yet it is exactly the kind of apparently far-fetched 'conceit', involving statements that seemed to generations of sober judges to be 'unnatural', which caused Donne's poetry, and poetry like it, to be so widely attacked in the century after his death, and caused Donne's own friend and contemporary Ben Jonson, a major critic, and a man in sympathy with Donne's work, to predict its failure to live; while to a mind like Dr. Johnson's, well-trained in almost everything but medieval theology, or to a Victorian mind, disciplined against wit and conceits and against all but the simplest types of religious emotion, such lines would seem to go beyond the bounds of taste and the orthodox function of poetic art. (It has become an English characteristic to dislike extravagance, cleverness, the outrageous, the hyperbolic, the paradoxical, and hence to dislike the ambivalences and ironies of the metaphysical style.) The death of Christ, in *Riding Westward*, is first stated, emotionally but with a complete and orthodox precision, as an almost impossible, a staggering world-contradiction: it is then described as an event in time producing (because it is an event of such extraordinary significance) extraordinary effects in the world of nature—

[1] i.e. life itself.

It made his owne Lieutenant Nature shrinke,
It made his footstoole crack and the Sunne winke.
Could I behold those hands which span the Poles,
And turn all spheares at once, pierc'd with those holes?
Could I behold that endlesse height which is
Zenith to us, and our Antipodes,
Humbled below us? . . .[1]

'. . . Now as from the sixth hour there was darkness over all the land . . . and the earth did quake and the rocks rent.' It is this tremendous interruption of nature, this 'spectacle of too much weight', that Donne has in mind as he rides into the setting sun. His achievement in the poem is, once again, to set vividly side by side the individual's experience, with its awareness of inadequacy, and the macrocosmic happenings with which he is obliged, as a Christian, to grapple, and with which he must somehow come to terms—though he can never perhaps quite assimilate them. This juxta-position of 'incompatible' scales in the unique compati-bility of Christianity is summed up in 'Could I behold that endless height which is Zenith to us . . .'

Walton can perhaps come to our rescue in summing up this poem, with a passage to be found in the 1670 edition of his *Life*, describing Donne's death:

> Being speechless, and seeing heaven by that illumination by which he saw it; he did (as Saint Stephen) look steadfastly into it, till he saw the Son of man standing at the right hand of God his Father; and being satisfied with this blessed sight, as his soul ascended and his last breath departed from him, he closed his own eyes. . . .

.   .   .   .

[1] Of these lines Gosse remarked, 'Nothing could be more odious'. Such a judgment helps us to remember that until about thirty years ago, the usual critical attitude to Donne was still, in essence, that of Johnson.

The longest of the religious poems, *The Litanie* (twenty-eight nine-line stanzas), was written in 1609, at a time of both physical and mental strain.

'Since my imprisonment in my bed,' wrote Donne to Sir Henry Goodyer, 'I have made a meditation in verse which I call a litanie. The word you know imports no other than supplication.' This letter, incidentally, shows that Donne's friends looked forward to manuscript copies of his compositions as they were written:

> Though a copy of [*The Litanie*] were due to you now, yet I am so unable to serve myself with writing it for you at this time (being some thirty staves of nine lines) that I must entreat you to take a promise that you shall have the first. . . .

His friends evidently did not relax their demands even for copies of a lengthy prose work, for the same letter refers to a book which must be *Biathanatos* 'of which it is impossible for me to give you a copy so soon, for it is not of much less than 300 pages'.

To return, however, to *The Litanie*: Donne strives to recommend the poem to Goodyer as a composition embodying that *via media* in religious doctrine most acceptable to Anglicans.

> That by which it will deserve best acceptation is, that neither the Roman Church need call it defective, because it abhors not the particular mention of the blessed Triumphers in heaven, nor the Reformed can discreetly accuse it of attributing more than a rectified devotion ought to do.

But despite this earnest and scrupulous advertisement of moderateness, *The Litanie*, with its passionate, rich, elaborately lilted and stressed stanzas, seems to belong less to meditative Anglican devotional verse than to the less urbane, more violent Catholic poetic tradition. Donne's first stanza is almost the poetry of a religious *aficionado*:

Father of Heaven, and him, by whom
It, and us for it, and all else, for us
Thou madest and govern'st ever, come
And re-create me now growne ruinous:
    My heart is by dejection, clay,
      And by selfe-murder, red.
From this red earth, O Father, purge away,
All vicious tinctures, that new fashioned
I may rise up from death, before I am dead.

It is interesting to set beside that splendid stanza, with its unashamed sense of self (self as something spoiled but important because of its awareness of divine origin and salvation), another stanza, in which once more the English language is magnificently forced to the task of passionate worship of a truly Catholic creator:

    Thou mastering me
  God! giver of breath and bread;
    World's strand, sway of the sea;
  Lord of living and dead;
Thou has bound bones and veins in me, fastened me flesh,
And after it almost unmade, what with dread,
    Thy doing: and dost thou touch me afresh?
Over again I feel thy finger and find thee.[1]

Gerard Manley Hopkins wrote his *Wreck of the Deutschland* in 1876. Yet the ex-Catholic Dean of St. Paul's and the Jesuit father, separated though they are by two and a half centuries, occasionally speak the same language. What is at first sight syntactically obscure and emotionally complex in each is, in each, the expression of a sense of being inextricably, almost dangerously, involved in God, and of a creative need to explore in words this sense of entanglement with God. Such a personal and at the same time hierarchic, elaborately formal, indeed part-medieval, religious feeling was possible to an English divine in the

---

[1] Reprinted by permission of the Oxford University Press.

still all but Catholic Church of England of the seventeenth century (only a century away from Rome). In the nineteenth century it was only possible to Catholics like Hopkins or Francis Thompson.

The Litanie, then, has some of Donne's most sumptuous verse. When merely describing the orders of the Church Triumphant, the angels, patriarchs and apostles, Donne yet manages to convey too his own satisfaction, as sensual as it is spiritual, with the eternal grandeur and power which is to be predicated of that Church:

> Therefore with thee triumpheth there
> A Virgin Squadron of white Confessors,
> Whose bloods betroth'd, not marryed were,
> Tender'd, not taken by those Ravishers.

And in the previous verse:

> And since thou so desirously
> Didst long to die, that long before thou could'st,
> And long since thou no more could'st dye,
> Thou in thy scatter'd mystique body wouldst
>   In Abel dye, and ever since
>   In thine; let their blood come
>   To begge for us, a discreet patience
> Of death, or of worse life. . . .

Donne's own rapturous contemplation of the great good luck men call death is not entirely without envy for One who, alone, could 'desirously long to die' without committing sin. *Contemptus mundi* best fits him, who, as *creator mundi*, knows and understands those feelings of humanity which prompt the cry

> For Oh, to some
> Not to be Martyrs, is a martyrdome.

After verse xiii, *The Litanie* passes from a celebration of the Church Triumphant to an account of the Church

Militant, man's needs on earth as expressed in prayer.
Some of Donne's hardest, clearest and finest thinking
goes into this part of the poem:

> From needing danger, to bee good,
> From owing thee yesterdays teares to day,
> From trusting so much to thy blood
> That in that hope, wee wound our soule away . . .
>
> That wee may change to evennesse
> This intermitting aguish Pietie;
> That snatching cramps of wickednesse
> And Apoplexies of fast sin, may die;
>   That musique of thy promises,
>   Nor threats in Thunder may
> Awaken us to our just offices . . .
>
> That learning, thine Ambassador,
> From thine allegeance wee never tempt,
> That beauty, paradises flower
> For physicke made, from poyson be exempt,
>   That wit, borne apt high good to doe,
>   By dwelling lazily
> On Natures nothing, be not nothing too,
> That our affections kill us not, nor dye. . . .

Donne speaks in other places of his immoderate thirst
for learning; his appetite for the sensual beauty of this
world was certainly not less than other men's; while
few could know more poignantly than himself how
evanescent empty wit can be. Did he not call his own
early secular verses 'evaporations'? Wit, he says here,
can do high good—is indeed naturally endowed with
the power to do good, provided that we do not 'seem
religious only to vent wit', and provided that wit does
not 'dwell lazily on Nature's nothing', i.e. on those
unimportant phenomena of the transitory world of
sense which it is so desperately hard not to make a fuss

about. Wit as the agent of high good, on the other hand, is 'wit' in the full philosophic seventeenth-century sense, as in Cowley's famous definition.

The Litanie makes a twofold plea—for moderation and for honesty. 'That our affections kill us not, nor dye': that wonderful line sums up the equal dangers of the Scylla of excessive affection and the Charybdis of lack of affection; while as for honesty, when we pray right, 'Thou in us dost pray'. When we pray right we ask deliverance from the occasions to sin which are nothing but occasions to deny God in us, a lie that can only be told by self-deceit.

Other human weaknesses identified in religious terms in *The Litanie* are: 'tempting Satan to tempt us'; 'indiscreet humility'; 'thirst or scorne of fame'. Most are either excesses or deficiencies of virtues which are only virtues if they keep their Aristotelian golden mean. The evils Donne lists might indeed be listed again, for they are with us still, though we have new names for them. But the modern poem would omit the words of hope and remedy with which each stanza ends, the 'Lord deliver us'. For all 'the troubles of our proud and angry dust', Donnes prescribes, not a can of ale, but the Christian cures of faith, humility, prayer. . . .

> O be thou nail'd unto my heart,
>   And crucified againe,
> Part not from it, though it from thee would part,
> But let it be, by applying so thy paine,
> Drown'd in thy blood, and in thy passion slaine.

The reader of such words may well feel that (to borrow from Walton) his soul's 'too much mixture with dross makes it unfit to judge of these high raptures and illuminations'. Of course, not all of the divine poems are either rapturous or illuminated: the con-

scientious versified doctrine of a poem like *The Lamen-
tations of Jeremy for the most part according to Tremelius*
is for the most part unreadable. But when Donne
writes in his own person about his own spiritual life,
'the emblem of Christ affixed to an anchor' is fully felt
and used with all its traditional imagery to illuminate
and universalize personal experience. Thus in the
magnificent *Hymn to Christ upon the author's last going
into Germany* (1619) the poet's crossing of the North
Sea is not less but more significant because seen as the
Christian's voyage 'towards home'. The sea itself, once
seen as a woman's tears, is now the emblem of Christ's
blood, the 'torne ship' the emblem of the ark of salvation. Donne starts with, and never loses sight of, his
own experience. The real is the emblem of the ideal:

> In what torne ship soever I embarke,
> That ship shall be my embleme of thy Arke;
> What sea soever swallow mee, that flood
> Shall be to mee an embleme of thy blood;
> Though thou with clouds of anger do disguise
> Thy face; yet through that maske I know those eyes,
> Which, though they turne away sometimes,
>   They never will despise.

Such poetry, anchored fast to the inexhaustible and
unchanging image ('I know those eyes') of a personal
saviour, achieves a profound strength and calm which
is lacking in much of the unpredictable secular verse.

PROSE WORKS

---

1. JUVENILIA

B Y the end of his life Donne had written, as satirist, controversialist and divine, far more prose than verse. His early prose is certainly less remarkable than his early verse, though amusing enough to read. It includes a few 'characters' or thumb-nail sketches, an essay on valour, and a collection of epigrams, 'Newes from the Very Countrey', on such inexhaustible topics as atheists, Jesuits, women, the Court and statesmen. Some of these trifles were printed in Donne's lifetime in editions of the popular Jacobean anthology *Overbury's Wife*.

A little more considerable are the short essays called *Paradoxes and Problemes*. Satirical and 'shocking', they were certainly written during the 1590's and are his earliest prose works. They were first printed in 1633,[1] two years after his death. During his lifetime, they doubtless circulated, like the early poems, in manuscript, and were considered, not least by their author, to be unsuitable for publication. Both their style and content are characteristic of the taste of the Elizabethan age, whose *literati* were much given to the game of constructing short pieces, in prose or verse, in which, by a rhetorical trick involving the use of homonymy, false

---

[1] Some more were printed in 1652, and another, discovered in manuscript, was printed by E. M. Simpson in 1927.

analogies, etc., an unexpected conclusion can be drawn out of apparently blameless premises. It is a game that was played by medieval writers and by Italian Renaissance poets. Often, the subject of the paradox is a reversal of a standard Renaissance tenet, e.g. 'that nature is our worst guide', or 'that the gifts of the body are better than those of the mind'. To take an example, in defending woman's inconstancy, Donne argues that those things in the natural world are superior which are most subject to change: the heavens, stars and moon, water flowing, air flying, time that 'staies not'. If 'gold that lyeth still, rusteth; water, corrupteth, aire, that moves not, poysoneth', why then should what is virtuous in these great elements be thought vicious in women? The counter-argument which ought to refute such absurdities is then introduced: 'because they deceive men', but is answered in its turn, not without some very attractive and eloquent writing ('every woman is a science,[1] for he that plods upon a woman all his life long shall at length find himself short of the knowledge of her: they are born to take down the pride of wit,') until the conclusion is reached that, if for inconstancy we admit the synonym 'variety', we shall see that a woman is the most delightful thing in the world.

This is rather trivial stuff, even when put beside its trivial poetic counterparts (e.g. *Womans Constancy* in *Songs and Sonets*), but the prose in which Donne serves it up is admirably light, easy and free from pompousness, while able at times to rise to a considerable and pointed eloquence as in the beginning of the fourth paradox ('that Good is more common than evil,' a 'serious' paradox): 'I have not been so pitifully tired with any vanity as with silly old mens exclaiming against these

[1] Cf. 'Women are like the arts', Elegy III, line 5.

times and extolling their own.[1] Alas! they betray them-selves: for if the times be changed their manners have changed them. But their senses are to pleasures as sick men's tastes are to liquors; for indeed no new thing is done in the world, all things are what and as they were, and good is as ever it was, more plenteous, and must of necessity be more common than evil, because it hath this for nature and perfection, to be common. It makes love to all natures, all, all effect it. . . . There shall be no time when nothing shall be good. It dare appear and spread, and glister in the world, but evil buries itself in night and darkness. . . .' So often in prose of this time, the tongue slips out of the cheek when we aren't looking.

The *Problemes* (which follow the *Paradoxes*) are in a similar style, though perhaps slightly more ribald, answering questions like 'Why doth the pox so much affect to undermine the nose?' 'Why die none for love now?' is easily answered, too: because women are easier to get, and because these latter times have pro-vided men with better means of destruction, viz. the pox, gunpowder, youthful marriage, religious contro-versies. These 'evaporations' are unimportant as literature yet they contain memorable phrases like 'kissing, the strange and mystical union of soules' (foreshadowing *The Extasie*) which occurs in *Paradox* 2 'that women ought to paint.' The ending of that paradox is worth quoting too: 'Love her who shows her great love to thee in taking this pains to seem lovely to thee.' It reveals the strong moral basis of even the most impu-dent Elizabethan prose.

[1] Donne has portrayed this type of silly old man in the person of the cuck-olded husband in the conversation-piece Elegy XIV, *A Tale of a Citizen and his Wife*: see above, p. 94.

2. BIATHANATOS

The ninth of Donne's paradoxes is called 'That only cowards dare dye', and contains the sentence 'death is the chosen refuge of cowards'—a tilt at Senecan stoicism. Many years later—probably about 1607 or 1608—he reverted to the theme of suicide as a serious moral problem, in a long scientific enquiry called *Biathanatos*, which is his first important prose work. It was of course too controversial to be published during his lifetime. Donne gives an account of it in a letter written in 1619 (shortly before his departure for Germany) to Sir Robert Ker, a letter which is of great interest as showing Dr. Donne's attitude to the writings of Jack Donne. He writes as follows:

> I had need to do somewhat towards you above my promises; how weak are my performances, when even my promises are defective. I cannot promise, no not in my own hopes, equally to your merit towards me. But beside the Poems of which you took a promise, I send you another book to which there belongs this history. It was written by me many years since, and because it is upon a misinterpretable subject, I have always gone so near suppressing it, as that it is only not burnt; no hand hath passed upon it to copy it, nor many eyes to read it: only to some particular friends in both universities, then when I writ it, I did communicate it. And I remember I had this answer, that certainly there was a false thread in it, but not easily found. Keep it I pray, with the same jealousie; let any that your discretion admits to the sight of it, know the date of it, and that it is a book written by Jack Donne and not by Dr. Donne. Reserve it for me if I live, and if I die, I only forbid it the press and the fire. Publish it not, but yet burn it not, and between those, do what you will with it.

The moderation and compromise of that letter are very Anglican. If it is contrasted with, for example, some of the letters written by the twentieth-century Catholic modernist George Tyrrell when he first began to encounter official opposition to his writings, it is not hard to isolate what in Donne's temperament inclined him to the greater privacy and personal freedom offered by Anglicanism: and it is interesting that, towards the end of the long, tragic struggle with orthodoxy that finally killed him in his forty-ninth year, Tyrrell began to look back with longing to the Anglican Church into which he had been born, but from which his intellectual inclinations had led him, as a young man, to serve a more exacting régime.

Donne's son,[1] whom Augustus Jessopp, the nineteenth-century Donnian, called a 'damned scoundrel', made an adroit acknowledgment of the letter to Ker, in his preface to the first (1646) edition of *Biathanatos*, where he wrote, *à propos* his father's having forbidden the book 'both the press and the fire', that 'neither had I subjected it now to the public's view but that I could finde no way to defend it from the one but by committing it to the other. . .' Doubtless the book, on its first appearance, had a considerable *succès de scandale*.

Nevertheless, it is difficult to avoid writing that almost everything, today, is interesting about *Biathanatos* except the work itself. So anxious was Donne to avoid those sensational aspects in which his subject abounded, that he seems to have gone to the opposite extreme. The treatise is exhaustive, learned and heavy with the weight of authorities. The triple argument that suicide is, in exceptional circumstances, justifiable under natural, civil and canon law, depends for its solidity on the

---

[1] Also John (1604–62). A brief account of his career is given in the *Dictionary of National Biography*, vol. xv, p. 234.

number of its witnesses and the elaboration of its historical fact. In neither of those respects does Donne's great reading let him down. The famous Preface indeed is interesting as autobiography: Donne confesses that he has often had the 'sickly inclination' to commit suicide, whether because of his Catholic upbringing, or because of a natural proneness to that particular pathway of sin. And the conclusion is revealing, too: Donne there admits that he has 'earnestly forbidden his discourse all dark and dangerous secessions and divertings into points of our free will and of God's destiny'; which is exactly why today *Biathanatos* seems so stodgy and remote in its terms, compared with other prose works where Donne can push his subject through more wholeheartedly. But the intellectual discipline and hard work it must have demanded were probably just what the author needed to save him from the 'sickly inclination' to which the melancholy of his Mitcham days must at times have driven him. And, after all, Donne was a great orthodox theologian but he was not a great ethical philosopher.

3. PSEUDO-MARTYR

This work, which appeared in 1610, is politico-religious and is concerned with the nature of authority in its two kinds, ecclesiastical and temporal. It attacks the Society of Jesus in particular, and the Roman Church in general, which is, says Donne, 'oppressed with such heapes of ashes and dead Doctrine, as this of temporall jurisdiction, so that divers other churches, which perchance were kindled at that, may burne more clearly and fervently than that from which they were derived'. Again like George Tyrrell three centuries later, Donne is deeply concerned at the way in which Rome has allowed

itself to fall victim to so many errors and follies that it
forces those who might have served it to protest and attack.

The argument of the work is that the Popes have so
usurped secular authority as to give 'pseudo-martyrs'
that contempt for it which makes them ready to covet
divine glory through secular treason (the commonest
way to martyrdom: Donne is trying to minimize such
deaths as Campion's). As regards Catholicism in England
Donne observes: 'Nor is it so harsh and strange as you
use to make it, that Princes should make it treason to
advance some Doctrines, though they be obtruded
as points of religion, if they involve sedition and ruine
or danger to the state; for the law says, that is *maiestatis
crimen* which is committed against the security of the
State, and in that place it calls securitie Tranquillitie.'
Donne speaks for the times, and for the State, and what
he says seems strikingly modern when one thinks of
contemporary political offenders, 'pseudo-martyrs' from
the point of view of national orthodoxy, who have
advanced their doctrines as points of a religion centred
in Moscow instead of Rome.

As for the Society of Jesus, its members' oath 'that
they shall return into England to preach the Catholique
faith publiquely there' is alluded to, as is also their
extremism—'this hunger of false-martyrdom goes ever
together with blasphemy against princes'. But there is
more than one flash of insight into those difficulties of
conscience which can be involved in any allegiance to a
secular power, as for example the observation that 'in
temporal monarchies the light of nature instructs every
man generally what treason is, that is, what violates or
wounds or impeaches the Maiestie of the State, and yet
he submits himself willingly to the Declaration and
Constitutions, by which some things are made to his
understanding treason, which by the general light he

apprehended not to be so dangerous before'—an observation that hardly needs underlining today.

The book was of course abused by the English Catholic party. One of its leaders, Thomas Fitzherbert, spoke caustically of Donne's 'superficial knowledge' and 'Lucianicall[1] and atheistical humour', and advised him to stick to 'his old occupation of making satires wherein he hath some talent and may play the fool without controle'. But in *Pseudo-martyr*, though working on commission (the book was written as propaganda when Donne was working for Morton and is dedicated to the King), he reaches considerable heights of eloquence, particularly when he has as his theme some universal subject, like man's soul: 'It is entire man that God hath care of, and not the soule alone, therefore his first worke was the body and the last worke shall be the glorification thereof.' The soul, says Donne, is God's and we should guard it carefully until it please Him 'to take home into his treasury this rich carbuncle our soule, which gives us light in our night of ignorance and our dark body of earth'. But we err if we make our soul 'so much our own that we may unthriftily spend it upon surfeits or licentiousness or reputation. From thence proceeds that corrupt prodigality of their lives with examples whereof all histories abound'—i.e. the pseudo-martyr commits an offence against a piece of God's property lent him by God to be guarded, if he 'in an immature and undigested zeale expose his life for testimony of a matter which were already believed, or to which he were not called by God'. It seems fair to say that the lawyer, and perhaps also the civil servant, in Donne, helped the theologian to find so effective a counterblast to the Catholic view of authority:

[1] This adjective seems more apt for *Ignatius His Conclave*, of which the fantastic setting and wit owe something to Lucian *via* such a work as Seneca's satire on the deification of the Emperor Claudius, the *Apocolocyntosis*.

that the master of language presided over its eloquent setting forth, is self-evident, even to those who would echo Ben Jonson's verdict on polemicists: 'these fencers in religion I like not'.

4. IGNATIUS HIS CONCLAVE

This brilliant satire against the Jesuits was written in 1610, and went through three editions in the following year. Two were in Latin, with the title 'Conclave Ignatii', the third in English. It must have been one of Donne's most popular works, and deservedly so: of all his controversial essays it is the one that can be read with the greatest pleasure today.

The presentation is through the device of a dream or vision. 'I was in an extasie,' writes Donne, 'and . . . had libertie to wander through all places. . . When I had surveyed all the heavens then . . . in the twinkling of an eye, I saw all the rooms in hell open to my sight.' In what follows, various candidates for hell present themselves to Lucifer. They are the great Renaissance heretic-innovators: Copernicus, Paracelsus, Macchiavelli. Copernicus pleads 'Shall these gates be open to such as have innovated in small matters, and shall they be shut against me, who have turned the whole frame of the world, and am thereby almost a new Creator?' It is here that Ignatius, founder of the Society of Jesus, is introduced as having got 'neere his [Lucifer's] chair, a subtil fellow and so indued with the Devil that he was able to tempt, and not only that, but (as they say) even to possess the Devil'.

Ignatius is shown 'opposing himself against all others' who seek admittance to hell, for fear that they may be dangerous competitors for the influence over Lucifer which he wishes to reserve for himself. The long speeches

of Macchiavelli, and Ignatius' answers, are interesting
for their full discussion of this most controversial figure
of the Renaissance who had such an effect on Elizabethan
thought. Much of the argument here is technical
theology, not political criticism: in addition, since
Donne's intention is to satirize the Jesuits, Ignatius'
refutation of, for instance, Macchiavelli's claim to have
'brought in the liberty of dissembling and lying' (the best-
known thing about him) must be taken ironically.

After Macchiavelli's discomfiture, Lucifer retires and
more or less leaves the interviewing to Ignatius. His
dismissal of Columbus is amusing and worth quoting:

> Nor did he use Christopher Columbus with any better res-
> pect who, having found all ways in the earth and sea open to
> him, did not fear any difficulty in hell, but when he offered
> to enter, Ignatius staid him and said 'You must remember
> sir, that if this kingdom have got anything by the discovery of
> the West Indies, all that must be attributed to our Order . . .
> and except we had been alwaies ready to convey and apply
> this medicine made of this precious American dung unto
> the princes of Europe . . . the profit by the onely[1] dis-
> covery of these places (which must of necessity be referred
> to fortune) would have been very little. Yet I praise your
> perseverance and your patience which (since that seems to
> be your principal virtue) you shall have good occasion to
> exercise here. . .'

In the end, Lucifer tries to get rid of Ignatius by
suggesting that he should emigrate to the moon and
found there a new hell: for lunatics like himself, presumably. But in the end, Ignatius' canonization is
announced (it was strictly beatification, and occurred
in 1609). This Roman practice is much mocked at by
Donne, who says it is 'now growne a kind of declaration
by which all men may take knowledge that such a one,

[1] i.e. 'mere'.

to whom the Church of Rome is much beholden, is now made partaker of the principal dignities and places in Hell'. So Ignatius gets his place and proceeds to evict from Lucifer's right hand Pope Boniface III, 'to whom as a principal innovator for having first challenged the name of universal Bishop, that honour was afforded'. But Ignatius makes short work of Boniface's claim, and Donne leaves the Jesuit enthroned with this concluding observation: 'how fitly and proportionately Rome and Hell answered one another, after I had seen a Jesuit turne the Pope out of his chaire in Hell, I suspected that that Order would attempt as much at Rome' (an allusion to the great power of the Society at that time).

The first edition of *Ignatius* appeared anonymously, the preface beginning, 'Doest thou seek after the Author? It is in vaine, for he is harder to be found than the parents of Popes were in the old times.' But no man then alive in England could have written it except Donne, and his authorship could—and need—have been no secret. Dazzlingly up-to-date in its acquaintance with astronomy and the new learning, at home with Jesuit casuistry and the practices of Rome, it is one of the cleverest polemics ever produced by an English theologian. And much of it is still entertaining even for non-theologians, as is no other of Donne's polemics. As an example of its humour, the tilt at plenary indulgences may be quoted. These, according to Donne, were given 'not only to the Franciscans themselves, but to their parents also, and to any which dyes in their habit; and to any which desire that they may do so; and to those who are wrapped in it after death, though they did not desire it'. Perhaps here, if not in *Pseudo-martyr*, Thomas Fitzherbert and the Catholic party would have been right to recognize Donne 'at his old occupation of making satires'.

5. ESSAYS IN DIVINITY

Though much less read than the *Devotions*, and, unlike them never published by Donne, the *Essays in Divinity* is one of his major works and is important as a solid balance to the more personal and romantically produced *Devotions*. In the *Essays*, written at some time during the five years before his ordination, Donne writes, as he himself says, as a 'vulgar Christian . . . in a low degree, but to my equals'. He recognizes at the same time, while indicating that his *Essays* do not satisfy it, a need for a 'metatheology and superdivinity, above that which serves our particular consciences', and thus makes it clear that here is no transcendental *vade-mecum* for the curious unbeliever, but merely a private attempt to set down the nature and meaning of the basic Christian ideas: the Creation of the World, and the Name, Word and Attributes of the Creator. It is an extensive theological commonplace book.

There are not many here of the purple patches one gets in the Sermons and *Devotions*. But because the *Essays* were written at an important period of Donne's life, to clarify his knowledge of the faith which he was soon openly to embrace, they are in a sense much more central to his position—as a theologian, not as an artist—than the *Devotions*. The reader who finds them hard going might perhaps be encouraged by some words of Ezra Pound in his *Guide to Kulchur*: 'Belief, as the pious once used the term, is alien to our age. We may have a respect for the unknown. We may have a pious disposition. We may have a wide sense of possibility. The child of the age is so accustomed to the loose waftiness of demoliberal ideology, that it takes sharp speech to open his mind to the thousand and more years of Europe, during which the intellectual hard work of the west occurred inside the Catholic Church.' It is that great millennium of intellectual hard work that Donne (living in the last decades of the pious but long before the birth of demo-liberalism) inherited. Though himself outside the Catholic Church, he had been brought up inside it, and he knew its teaching thoroughly and, like all Anglicans, approved of three-quarters of that teaching. Besides the Scriptures themselves, his theological writings draw freely on the early Latin Fathers, on Aquinas and on the medieval and Renaissance commentators of every country of the West. He still sees that intellectual hard work as an important, valid—indeed, essential—basic achievement which he, drawn by temperament and circumstance into the profession of Christian theologian, must assimilate and interpret.

The *Essays* then, cannot be disguised as superdivinity, but must be read 'straight' as they were written straight. There is no *mystique* in them, and hardly anything of the loneliness or agony of religious struggles. On the contrary, the emphasis is throughout joyfully placed on the great open thesaurus of shared Christian teaching, on the sense of God's work and work as the common inheritance of the then civilized world, in which all minds will be glad to move with interest and wonder. Much of the book is hard-going exposition, packed with authorities both quoted and alluded to: Donne's mind is too alert, too personally concerned about religion, to remain aloof. That is why the argument is so closely-knit. No difficulty or possibility is shirked, no argument cut short, no relevant detail omitted.

Two examples may be given, one small and one great, of the personal touch of the English writer manifesting itself in a book the body of which belongs to European theology more than to English literature. In discussing excess of charity, Donne makes his point with a very concrete comparison, an image of English rural life: 'And therefore, as waggoners in steep descents tie the team behind, not to draw it up, but to stop sudden precipitations downwards, so, only to prevent such slippery downfalls, I say, that as the Holy Ghost forbids *Be not just overmuch*, so one may be charitable overmuch.' Secondly, the whole long and rather tedious narration of the Exodus is 'paraphrased' (i.e. *applied* to the contemporary perpetual need of mankind for deliverance from sin, according to the theological idea that the literal statements in the Bible are not only true *per se* but true also as parable or prophecy, timelessly as well as historically true) in one of the finest and most personal passages in the book, a smiting of the dry rock to produce the water of life. 'Dig a little deeper, oh my poor lazy soul, and thou shalt see that thou and all mankind are delivered from an Egypt and more miraculously than these [i.e. the Jews],' it begins, and then the poet's fire kindles the theologian's earnestness:

And then camest thou, O Christ, thine own Moses, and deliveredst us; not by doing but suffering, not by killing but dying. Go one step lower, that is higher and nearer to God, O my soul, in this Meditation, and thou shalt see, that even in this moment when he affords thee these thoughts, he delivers thee from an Egypt of dulness and stupidity. . . Thou hast delivered me, O God, from the Egypt of confidence and presumption, by interrupting my fortunes and intercepting my hopes; and from the Egypt of despair by contemplation of thine abundant treasures, and my portion therein; from the Egypt of lust, by confining my affections and from the monstrous and unnaturall Egypt of painful and wearisome idleness, by the necessities of domestick and familiar cares and duties.

Perhaps the corner-stone of the theological structure of the *Essays* is Donne's 'consideration of God'. It is a simple, cogent, beautifully controlled piece of writing, anchoring the Christian upon faith not upon reason, and employing the characteristic geographical images of voyaging and discovery.

> Men which seek God by reason and natural strength (though we do not deny common notions and general impressions of a sovereign power) are like Mariners which voyaged before the invention of the compass, which were but coasters, and unwillingly left the sight of the land. Such are they which would arrive at God by this world, and contemplate him only in his Creatures, and seeming Demonstration. Certainly, every creature shews God as a glass, but glimmeringly and transitorily by the frailty both of the receiver, and beholder: Our selves have his Image as Medals, permanently and preciously delivered. But by these meditations we get no further, than to know what he *doth*, not what he *is*. But as by the use of the compass, men safely dispatch Ulysses' dangerous ten years travel in so many days and have found out a new world richer than the old; so doth Faith, as soon as our hearts are touched with it, direct and inform us in that great search of the discovery of God's essence, and the new *Hierusalem* which Reason durst not attempt. And though the faithfullest heart is not ever directly and constantly upon God, but that it sometimes descends also to reason; yet it is not thereby so departed from him, but that it still looks towards him, though not fully to him: as the compass is ever northward, though it decline and have often variations towards East and West.

Now and again there is a pause in the argument, and Donne interpolates a prayer, as if for guidance and refreshment before continuing his task (four additional prayers are printed at the end of the work). One of the finest of these prayers opens with the words 'O Eternal and Almighty Power, which being infinite, hast enabled a limited creature, faith, to comprehend thee,' providing

in its humility a contrast to the intellectual complexities
of the *Essays* proper.

In the *Essays* Donne is struggling with definitions,
with fixities, with the whole vast literature of medieval
theology. Into its propositions and controversies he
entered with zest and skill. Once again, Ezra Pound
may remind us that in the best age of scholastic thought
(at the end of which Donne stands, and to the fruits of
which he had continual access) the ecclesiastical doctors
took care of their terminology because they had 'almost
nothing but words to deal with'. Modern writers, with
the exception of logical positivist philosophers, tend
to take less care over terminology and are less interested
in the art of definition. Pound constantly emphasizes
the important fact that most of us, when it comes to
coping with medieval and Renaissance writing, are not
educated. We educate ourselves by reading Donne,
but we do not read his source-material: we omit those
writers and techniques which educated him. 'Lawyers,'
writes Donne in the third part of *Essays in Divinity*, (and
he should have known), 'more than others have ever
been tyrants over words and have made them accept
other significations than their natures inclined to'.
Nowadays, words tend to tyrannize over us instead.
Medieval lawyers could play deliberate tricks with
meanings, knowing what those meanings should be.
Lacking, often, that basic knowledge, we allow meanings
to become blurred and confused and imprecise. We
are technically ill-equipped to read books like Donne's
Essays: we are too lazy to follow the arguments, which
we find dull and dead: arguments as arguments, words
forced to do battle for the sake of righteousness, these
no longer appeal to us. Open the *Essays* and come upon
this, for example: 'Propagation is the truest image and
nearest representation of Eternity.' This proposition

Donne now proceeds to explain, justify and elaborate: 'For Eternity itself, that is, the Deity itself, seems to have been ever delighted with it: for the producing of the three persons in the Trinity, which is a continuing and undeterminable work, is a propagation of the Deity.' Without faith, there could be no theological mind, but once grounded in faith, the theological mind will delight to move by logic.

But for the last hundred and fifty years it has been easier to appreciate such a statement as 'Truly the Creation and the Last Judgment are the *Diluculum* and *Crepusculum*, the Morning and the Evening twilights of the long day of this world,' than to follow a discussion on the propriety and meaning of 'Omnipotent' as an attribute of God. It is easier to let our minds become charged with the grandeur of the first verse of Genesis than to follow an exegesis upon that verse. The vaguer, more romantic phrases of divinity—'in the beginning was the Word', 'the long day of this world'—do not insist on being precisely defined. They are appeals to our emotions, gestures towards the unknown. But in the *Essays in Divinity* Donne, as a professional theologian, comes to grips with religion as a system of thought. The man of the Renaissance, the dweller in the bright shadow of the new learning, must discipline himself to travel, though at a late hour, through the complicated medieval universe of his God.

6. DEVOTIONS

Donne's *Devotions upon emergent occasions* has probably been the most widely read of his prose works. It consists of twenty-three groups of essays, each group containing a meditation, an 'expostulation' and a prayer, and each taking as its text one of the stages of the violent fever with which Donne was confined to bed during the winter of 1623–4. These stages, from the disease's first sudden assault down to the beginning of con- valescence, Donne lists at the beginning of the book in a series of twenty-two Latin hexameters which have all the fascination of a seventeenth-century medical case. That is the framework: but the heart of the work is Donne's faith that (to quote from one of his sermons) 'God will make a feaver speak to me, and tell me his mind, that there is no health but in him.'

The *Devotions* is no secret 'revelation', nor is it a manuscript left behind by a dead man. Donne recovered from his illness, and in the spring of 1624 revised the work and had it printed—one of the very few of his works that was published during his lifetime. We must expect, then, a work of which its author himself must have thought highly, a work of orthodox Christian piety. Yet it may not be fanciful to believe the earlier passages, inspired by the first stages of illness and so, naturally, springing from a powerful awareness of the possibility of death, to be more 'interesting' and more original than the expressions of thanksgiving and resolu- tion with which the book ends. Nevertheless, we should regard Donne's fever as he himself did, as a convenient and timely symbol of human imperfection from which we may be given—indeed are given—the chance of rescue. Deprived of health of body, which stands, after all, for those countless opportunities to sin, the soul can come into its own.

Thus it is as a record of a Christian soul 'coming into its own,' free from the body precisely because the body is not free, that the *Devotions* is of value and interest. In a sermon preached at Lincoln's Inn Donne said of sickness 'In poverty I lack but other things; in banish- ment I lack but other men; but in sickness I lack myself.'

Though when writing the *Devotions* Donne was, as we say now, 'not himself', he was yet, in a sense, then most himself. 'Lacking himself' (i.e. all those distractions and occasions for false hope and pride which crowd upon us when we are well) he was the nearer to himself in his proper essence, a being fashioned to be able to contemplate God. He could examine the absent self, the old Adam, and be the better prepared to recognize and combat its follies when it returned to him.

The *Devotions*, while thus ranking high in England's great literature of spiritual exercise, yet possesses an extraordinary and important objectivity: Donne retains in it all his great powers of analysis and analogy, of being interested in what he feels and knows—but the characteristic Donnian wit is subdued and there is none of the old irony. The new quality which ousts that irony, and which is also operative in the religious poems, is a passionate humility which, being highly personal, being a profoundly arrived at and positive sense of human inadequacy, is more impressive—especially to a modern reader with little real religious experience—than the conventional Old Testament attitude of unreasoned, emotional self-abasement before an unknown or dimly apprehended God. Donne's life as a religious writer is a continuous *knowing* of God. His thought and feeling are essentially New Testament: his sense of man's position in the universe is upheld and realized by a constant emphasis upon Christ as the mediator between the human self and its God.

The prose of the great seventeenth-century English religious writers (Donne, Traherne, Andrewes, Taylor) being persuasive, its technique is naturally that of rhetoric. Yet the most characteristic tone of the *Devotions* is a curiously personal, almost intimate one— it is not unrhetorical altogether, but rather seems to

M

be private rhetoric: it is as if Donne were working emotionally upon his own thoughts, seeking to persuade them to take shape. Donne is after all not directly exhorting any congregation, as in his sermons: though undoubtedly, in issuing his 'most secret thoughts, his soul paraphrased' to the public, he meant to have his proper pastoral effect upon readers as upon listeners. Still, a man can be at his most universal when he most forgets other men and most concentrates on himself and on his personal relationship with God. For example, we feel the same pleading desire for identification with God in this—'How fully O my abundant God, how gently O my sweet my easy God, doest thou entangle me'—as in the *Holy Sonnets*. Generalizations will suffice for the multitude: but the heart that whispers to God needs another eloquence and a different kind of rhetoric. Again, in the 19th *Expostulation*, Donne seems to be offering up private images like sacrifices: the whole of his literary experience goes into this vivid attempt to make himself realize the nature of God:

> My God, my God, Thou art a direct God, may I not say a literall God, a God that wouldest be understood literally, and according to the plaine sense of all that thou sayest? But thou art also (Lord I intend it to thy glory, and let no profane misinterpreter abuse it to thy diminution) thou art a figurative, a metaphoricall God too: A God in whose words there is such a height of figures , such voyages, such peregrinations to fetch remote and precious metaphors, such extentions, such spreadings, such curtains of Allegories, such third heavens of Hyperboles, so harmonious eloquutions, so retired and so reserved expressions, so commanding persuasions. . . .

As so often happens, when the intellectual (even the devoutest one) describes his God, he slips into a description of himself. Here Donne paints God somewhat in his own image, yet who shall say that theology becomes thereby the loser to psychology, or that the two are not, in Donne, one?

There are in the *Devotions* many self-searchings and revelations of Donne's own fears, regrets and awareness of error. He speaks of 'the shadowes which doe fall upon me, faintnesses of spirit and condemnations of myself'. He prays to be delivered from 'these vaine imaginations'; for 'it is an overcurious thing, a dangerous thing, to come to that tenderness, that rawness, that scrupulousness, to fear every concupiscence, every offer of sin, that this suspicious and jealous diligence will turne to an inordinate dejection of spirit'. There can be little doubt that Donne never quite forgot the terror of that state of depression into which he fell so often during the years 1602–15. He seems to seek a point of balance between too much and too little sense of sin, between the pride of self-righteousness and the pride of self-destruction.

In a great passage on the text 'the doctors find the disease to steal on insensibly, and endeavour to meet with it so', Donne speaks of 'secret disobediences' against God and 'secret repugnances against his declared will'. Throughout the work the body's sickness symbolizes 'our soul's sicknesses which are sins'. So at this stage of the disease, when 'that which is most secret is most dangerous', the *Expostulation* (No. 10) is against the serpent in Eden, arch-symbol of all secret sin. 'In his curse, I am cursed too; his creeping undoes me. . . He works upon us in secret, and we doe not discern him; And one great worke of his upon us, is to make us so like himself as to sin in secret, that others may not see us. But his Masterpiece is, to make us sin in secret so, as that we may not see ourselves sin. . . . The bodie, the sinne, is the Serpents, and the garment that covers it, the lye, is his too.' There is a hint, too, of personal recollections of struggle against orthodoxy in 'Keepe me back, O Lorde, from them who mis-professe arts of healing the soule or of the body by means not imprinted by thee in the Church. . . . There is no spiritual health to be had by superstition, nor bodily by witchcraft,' as well as a general warning; and in writing such a pithy and memorable piece of wisdom as 'Some men give not their fruits but upon impor-tunitie', did Donne think wryly of his own recalci-trance during those vainly importunate years before 1615?

As in the *Devotions* sickness throughout stands for sin, so recovery stands for redemption, and, at the close of the sequence, the fear of a relapse stands for the fear of falling back into sin. This device of letting a thing stand both for itself and for some corresponding thing on a different, higher plane, is a familiar one in all medieval thought. We saw Donne using it in some of his secular poems in a far more free, fanciful and (the word is not meant to be derogatory) irresponsible way. In theology, such correspondences are highly organized throughout the writings of the great exegetical authori-ties. Donne, as a responsible theologian, takes over orthodox interpretations but still allows his mind to develop them in its own peculiar way. Thus, sleep stands for death: 'as then we need sleep to live out our three score and ten years, so we need death, to live that life which we cannot outlive'. And in another passage, 'Every night's bed is a type of the grave,' we are reminded of that sombre passage at the beginning of the Elegy on Lord Harington:

> when the labourers have
> Such rest in bed, that their last Church-yard grave,
> Subject to change, will scarce be'a type of this. . . .

But Donne, unlike the condemned man in his own poem, cannot 'practice dying by a little sleepe'. For he says that his sickness prevents him from sleeping, and turns this characteristically into a small, wry conceit, that his insomnia is 'an argument that Thou wouldest not have me sleep in Thy presence'.

There are several such conceits of the metaphysical kind in the *Devotions*, as in all the prose of that time. 'How ruinous a farme hath man in taking himself?' is typical; or a man departing from God's way is likened, in an image frequently found in Donne, to a man who, drawing a circle with a compass, removes the compass with the circle still uncompleted. And in a vivid passage, after he has heard the bell toll for a funeral, he asks 'If he who, as this bell tells me, is gone now, were some excellent artificer, who comes to him for a clock or for a garment now? or for counsell, if he were a lawyer? If a magistrate, for justice?' One could almost go straight on, using the words of another writer not many years earlier: 'Where be his quiddities now, his quillities, his cases, his tenures and his tricks?'[1]

The tolling of the funeral bell which Donne hears through the window of his sick-room, provides him with the occasion for what is undoubtedly the most impressive passage, the climax, of the emotional argument of the *Devotions*. He himself seems to recall it later, in a sermon preached in 1628: 'Is there any man,' he asked his congregation, 'that in his chamber hears a bell toll for another man, and does not kneel down to pray for that dying man? and then when his charity breaths out upon another man, does he not also reflect upon himself, and dispose himself as if he were in the state of that dying man?' What Donne preached in 1628 he had himself practised in 1623. He returns constantly in all his

---

[1] *Hamlet*, v, i.

writings to the idea that man is a world. He admits the usefulness to him of this concept in the 8th *Meditation*: 'Still when we return to that Meditation, that Man is a world, we find new discoveries. Let him be a world, and himself will be the land, and misery the sea.' To this geographical image Donne will return, but first he turns aside to a different image drawn from his own world of books and scholarship and developing out of the two senses in which the word 'author' can be used (i.e. in its general religious sense of creator, as in 'Author of peace and lover of concord', and in its limited literary sense). This passage on universal resurrection is of great beauty, but certainly achieves its remarkable effect through the exactness which sustains every phrase of the long, extended metaphor:

> All mankinde is of one Author, and is one volume; when one Man dies, one Chapter is not torn out of the booke but translated into a better language; and every Chapter must be so translated. God emploies several translators; some peeces are translated by age, some by sickness, some by warre, some by justice; but Gods hand is in every translation; and his hand shall binde up all our scattered leaves againe, for that Librarie where every booke shall lie open to one another.

It is here that Donne returns to his geographical image of the world and concludes his great statement that we are all connected by being the work of a single creator, all equal by being parts of that creator's total universe. 'No man is an Island, intire of it selfe; Every man is a peece of the Continent, a part of the maine. If a Clod bee washed away by the Sea, Europe is the lesse, as well as if a Promontorie were . . . any mans death diminishes me, because I am involved in Mankinde. And therefore never send to know for whom the bell tolls: It tolls for thee.'

'Because I am involved in Mankinde': there is the essential greatness of Donne and the essential challenge of the Age of Theology—the personal and the universal statement are one. In what contrast is that isolation of the heart which the Romantic and post-romantic poets preach, as they proclaim the irremediable aloneness of man and turn the image in reverse:

> Yes! in the sea of life enisled. . . .
> We mortal millions live *alone*.

Arnold, prophet of modern *angst*, essays a Donnian image of man as a world: but in his doubting hands the image suffers death by water, and we feel, in that hyper-poetical 'enisled', that in his sadness Arnold can only point vaguely at the sea as at something larger than himself. He cannot connect because he cannot surrender to the idea of a connecting God: and his inability to connect the hopelessly complex and disparate parts of the enormous unhappy jigsaw puzzle of the Victorian world leaves him lost and isolated. There is nothing of this romantic humanism in Donne's affirmation 'I am involved in mankind.' The statement is set far apart, by its passionate logic and coherence, from the tentative, negative suggestion of Arnold. Donne is no philan-thropic Victorian 'liberal humanist': he does not say 'all men are brothers', which, by itself, simply means 'if everyone was kind, tolerant, etc., like me, everything would be all right'. Donne does not dwell in a moral Utopia, but gives us his all-important logical *reason*s for claiming to be involved in mankind. It is, that 'all mankind is of one author'. It is this proposition which gives the claim 'I am involved in mankind' all its authority and significance. Theology makes, upon the mind of a writer like Donne, the psychological demands of an exact science. It contains no wishful thinking. Given its basic creed, there will follow chapter and verse for statements of the greatest magnitude and power which, if a humanist made them, would have to be taken on trust. They are, for example, thus taken in Tennyson's *In Memoriam*, in such a passage as

> . . . . . call
> To what I feel is Lord of all
> And faintly trust the larger hope.

Faith, trust, hope, somehow, faintly, falter: these are the vague, tentative, uncertain key-words of *In Memoriam*, a poem in which statements are regressively qualified until they almost resign the struggle to state, almost reach—for all their eloquence—the inarticulateness of

> An infant crying for the light:
> And with no language but a cry.

Tennyson's great poem enshrines a spiritual attitude which is the reverse of Donne's, and this is reflected in its vocabulary, which even when it describes attempts at faith is the vocabulary of doubt. Donne, even when he is recording his doubts and failures, uses the vocabulary of faith. Tennyson constantly uses the word 'hope,' which is rare in Donne.

Not all of the *Devotions* can so engage us. Sometimes we feel Donne has failed to control his 'vaine imagination'; sometimes he offers conceits as obvious and far-fetched to our taste as they would have been to Dr. Johnson's: 'There is more fear, therefore more cause. . . There is a growth of the disease then. But there must be an autumn too. But whether an autumn of the disease or mee, it is not my part to choose. But if it be of me, it is of both. My disease cannot survive me, I may overlive it' (7th *Meditation*). There are similar passages in many of the Sermons. Coleridge in his *Notes on*

English Divines quotes one of them: 'What is this enemy? an enemy that may thus far think himself equal to God, that as no man ever saw God and lived, so no man ever saw this enemy and lived: for it is death'— and neatly hits off its slightly ludicrous wit by saying that it 'borders rather too closely on the Irish Franciscan's conclusion to his sermon of thanksgiving: "Above all, brethren, let us thankfully laud and extol God's transcendent mercy in putting death at the end of life, thereby giving us all time for repentance."'

Yet in that 7th *Meditation*, which begins so unpromisingly, there later occurs a piece of strong, supple prose, full of weight, rhythm and evocative truth, an unexpected reward for perseverance. 'Death is in an old man's dore, he appears and tells him so: and death is at a young man's back, and says nothing. Age is a sickness, and youth is an ambush; and we need so many phisicians as may make up a watch, and spie every inconvenience. There is scarce anything that hath not killed somebody.' Such diction, lying somewhere between homeliness and studied simplicity, has a masculine directness that is wholly typical of Donne's mind, though we are rarely allowed to see it so unadorned. Simple and almost conversational, these passages are like some of the openings of the *Songs and Sonets*.

But generally the texture of Donne's prose is richer and more elaborate than that—for example, the wonderful passage on light in the 14th Prayer, or that on the heart of man ('they use cordials to keep the venim and malignity of the disease from the heart') where he dwells on his key-word—'how little of man is the heart, and yet it is all by which he is'—with all the pleading music of the artist and the lover of man. 'Hearts, not so perfect as to be given but that the very giving mends them; not so desperate as not to be accepted, but that the very accepting dignifies them. This is a melting heart and a troubled heart and a wounded heart and a broken heart and a contrite heart. . . .' The word moves through infinite risings and fallings of sadness and solace: it is a word Jack Donne juggled with more than once in *Songs and Sonets*. But when the Dean, whose own heart is full of the experiences of his own life, takes up the word again, it no longer 'evaporates' into airy wit; it is no longer the heart of some mocked and mocking Ovidian lover: it is the heart of man. Irony cannot enter, for there is no room. Donne is not hiding behind any *persona* or mask, but is speaking of himself, with no reserve, to God. 'By the powerful working of thy piercing spirit, such a heart I have.'

The secular wit, the humanist's irony and cynicism so markedly lacking in the *Devotions* were discarded by Donne along with his secular *weltanschauung* and the pro-fane poems of his early life. Irony is a weapon, a *modus operandi* of the mind prone to 'vaine imagination', the mind that is trying to keep its balance in a world whose complexity seems to demand a defensive attitude which, in religion, is impossible. It belongs to the 'cold melan-choly' of Donne's temperament during the years when, though on the whole physically hale, he was psychologi-cally ill-at-ease, uncertain of the future, disillusioned with the present, and balanced on irony as on a fence separating hope from despair. He writes indeed, at the very beginning of the *Devotions* (on the miserable condi-tion of humanity), of his body's sickness as a natural fever and his mind's melancholy as an unnatural one. Religious meditation is here made to drive out the 'unnatural'.

But Donne is still not free of one temptation which we know to have been strong in him in earlier years: a fas-cination and preoccupation with death. Not that any-where in the *Devotions* he allows himself to brood on the physical horror of death as he does in some of the *Sermons*.

Rather he returns sometimes, longingly yet timidly, like a child almost, to the idea of death. 'Death destroys a man, but the idea of death saves him,' wrote E. M. Forster; and in the tolling of the passing-bell there came to Donne the inexorable idea of death. For it is the death of mankind for which the bell tolls, that death of Adam symbolized once for all upon the cross and renewed by the death of every man that dies. 'Christ', says Donne, 'is my Master in this Science of Death'; one feels him trying to push the idea of death out of the realm of unnatural cold melancholy into the natural realm, its proper place in the Christian's world, where it is that which, destroying the body, releases the soul. During the dark years at Mitcham, Donne was obsessed with thoughts of suicide. Now as a minister of God, he has fought that temptation, not without glory, but has, perhaps, legitimized rather than overcome it. Indeed, who is to draw the line between desire for death as a sin, a rejection of our lot upon earth, and acceptance of death as a virtue, a rejection of our fear of extinction? 'If man knew', Donne writes in the 16th *Meditation*, 'the gaine of death, the ease of death, he would solicit, he would provoke death to assist him by any hand which he might use. But as when men see many of their own professions preferred, it ministers a hope that that may light upon them; so when these hourly bells tell me of so many funerals of men like me, it presents, if not a desire that it may, yet a comfort whensoever mine shall come.'

That is a most revealing and interesting passage. I suppose it would take a theologian to pronounce a verdict on the question whether Donne quite excuses himself with that phrase 'if not a desire that it may'. I think at least it cost Donne an effort of will, a sacrifice of his psychological independence, to face death without either terror or desire, but neutrally, with perfect orthodoxy. And I do not think he quite succeeds in that effort, nor quite makes that sacrifice. He refers to death as 'preferment': for him it is a release, a return home. For a sick man, growing old (fifty to a man of Donne's time was much older than it seems nowadays) *contemptus mundi* is natural, not unnatural. And death then is more easily seen, as a Christian ought presumably to see it after all, as the end of a life which being sinful and corrupt is no life at all in the sense in which Christ used the word when he said 'I am the Resurrection and the Life'.

Perhaps, then, one could argue that Donne speaks of death in the *Devotions* neither hysterically nor with any unnatural longing, but simply as God's natural and blessed limitation placed upon man's otherwise endless power to sin. He refuses to emotionalize the corruption of the body or to be over-rhetorical about the bliss of the soul after death. Those splendid excesses of hell and heaven he leaves to the sermons. They were not wasted, it is certain, upon his vast and appreciative congregations: but, perhaps, in his own physical crisis, they would have been wasted on himself. Instead, he prays, simply and unexceptionably: 'Let this prayer therefore, O my God, be as my last gasp, my expiring, my dying in thee; That if this bee the hour of my *Transmigration* I may die the death of a sinner, drowned in my sins, in the blood of thy sonne. And if I live longer, yet I may now die the death of the righteous, die to sinne, which death is a resurrection to a new life. Thou killest and thou givest life.'

Does, then, the metaphysical poet have the last word? Or, rather, does the Christian prepare for both worlds, with only the cynic objecting ' the *best* of both worlds'? I do not believe Donne deceived himself, and in the *Devotions* he had no public, set task to fulfil—other, of course, than to see that the world did not receive heresies as the private thoughts of the Dean of St. Paul's. Looking into his own heart, looking back on his own life, Donne knew that he was also looking into many hearts and back into many lives: he knew that the world of man, 'yea the great globe itself', was corrupt, and that this corruption was readily symbolized in the sickness of his own body. He knew too, that as he himself recovered from sickness, so the soul of man would rise again at the last day. 'And that as thou hatest sin itself, thy hate to sin may be expressed in the abolishing of all instruments of sin, the allurements of this world *and the world itself.*' For the humanist, man is the measure of good, and such a plea for destruction would be dismissed easily enough. But Donne has more to say: 'If I were but mere dust and ashes, I might speak unto the Lord, for the Lord's hand made me of this dust, and the Lord's hand shall recollect these ashes. . . But I am more than dust and ashes; I am my best part, I am my soule. And being the breath of God, I may breathe back these pious expostulations to my God.'

The humanist can but make the most of time: Donne, as a Christian, must pray instead 'that Time may be swallowed up in eternity and hope swallowed in possession and ends swallowed in infiniteness and all men ordained to salvation'. No modern reader who reads even a small part of the *Devotions* can fail to be struck with the sense of there being two worlds, the corrupt world of man, our temporal world, subject to sickness and death, and the perfect world of God, to which our souls, being of God, aspire and which in part they symbolize—the world of eternity. Donne's prose is the prose of a man at home in both worlds, of a man who lived before the era of enlightenment came to separate these worlds. Once again, it is Matthew Arnold who best expresses the result of this separation, when he speaks of

> Wandering between two worlds, one dead,
> The other powerless to be born . . .

But in Donne's time the two worlds were both alive and integrated with each other, and man was not a wanderer but a being with a purpose, whose uniqueness Sir Thomas Browne summed up when he called him 'that great and true Amphibium'.

7. 'A PREACHER IN EARNEST'

For the last sixteen years of his life, the whole—or nearly the whole—of Donne's literary output was in the form of sermons. He was, says Walton, 'a preacher in earnest, weeping sometimes for his Auditory, sometimes with them: always preaching to himself, like an angel from a cloud, but in none; carrying some, as St. Paul was, to Heaven in holy raptures, and enticing others by a sacred art and courtship to amend their lives; here picturing a vice so as to make it ugly to those that practised it; and a virtue so, as to make it be beloved even by those that loved it not; and all this with a most particular grace and an unexpressible addition of comeliness'.

But the grace, the comeliness, the tears, the voice and the gestures, are indeed unexpressible now, and we are left with the impossible task of reconstructing them from cold and dusty print. More than a hundred and fifty sermons of Donne's were published during the seventeenth century, although only six appeared in print in his lifetime, and few of his admirers are likely to have either the time or the inclination to read very far into this formidable output. Today the Church of England is still important for state and social occasions, but it no longer represents a major force in the community of the nation. In the general defeat of personal contact and corporate life which began fifty years ago and has been increased by mechanical pseudo-contacts available in the home, what victim is more pathetic than the Anglican Church and what symbol more wretched than the studio congregation of a broadcast service, going to church on behalf of millions who will never go again till the bell tolls for them and for them alone?

Of course, great preachers are rare in any age and preachers of great literary gifts even rarer. But a church in its golden age will at least provide the climate in which good preaching can flourish. Sermons were not yet, in the seventeenth century, mere appendices to the service book, but separate events often taking place outside the service and outside the church: they lasted much longer than any modern sermon—an hour and a half would not have been thought exceptional—and offered the church its opportunity to employ popular rhetoric. Donne's congregations were as ready to listen to him in the cold London air of Paul's cross[1] as in the cathedral itself; and besides addressing the citizens of London, he could vary his approach to create an impact on a professional audience at Lincoln's Inn or a royal one at Whitehall, where the sermon was often a command performance.

In Donne's time, the old order was slowly changing: could he have prophesied that less than twenty years after his death the monarchy itself would be overthrown? ' 'Tis all in pieces, all cohaerence gone.' But still the divine order of the macrocosm could come to the rescue

---

[1] This ancient London meeting-place was outside the north-east corner of the old cathedral—the pulpit, according to Dean Milman, not only of St. Paul's but of the Church of England. It was destroyed during the Civil War.

of the disordered 'little kingdom' of man: still, then, the 'poore riddling, perplexed labyrinthical soule' of the unbeliever was thought to be only temporarily lost, was still offered rescue and—more urgent—reasons why it should surrender to its rescuer. And the lost soul had only one rescuer to turn to, the Christian Church. After all, even in an age of faith there will be many—and often the most gifted will be among them— who will find it hard to believe, hard to surrender their chaos for order, their private uncertainty for a common reconciliation. But they will, in an age of faith, be unable to avoid the *possibility* of belief. They will understand the idea of belief and the desire to believe. It is interesting to see what Donne had to say to the unbeliever, and to see his method of saying it, in the sermon he preached at St. Paul's on 25 January, 1629:

> Poor intricated soul! Riddling perplexed labyrinthical soule! Thou couldest not say that thou believest not in God if there were no God. Thou couldest not believe in God if there were no God. If there were no God, thou couldest not speak, thou couldst not think, not a word, not a thought, no not against God. Thou couldest not blaspheme the Name of God, thou couldest not sweare, if there were no God. For all thy faculties however depraved and perverted by thee, are from him, and except thou canst seriously believe that thou art nothing, thou canst not believe that there is no God. If I should ask thee at a tragedy, where thou shouldest see him that had drawn blood, lie weltering and surrounded in his owne blood, 'Is there a God now?' If thou couldst answer me, 'No, these are but Inventions, and Representations of men, and I believe a God never the more for this;'—If I should ask thee at a sermon, where thou shouldst hear the judgments of God formerly denounced and executed, re-denounced and applied to present occasions, 'Is there is a God now?' If thou couldest answer me, 'No, these are but Inventions of state, to souple and regulate

Congregations, and keep people in order, and I believe a God never the more for this'; Bee as confident as thou canst, in company; for company is the Atheists Sanctuary; I respite thee not till the day of judgment, when I may see thee upon thy knees, upon thy face, begging of the hills that they would falle down and cover thee from the fierce wrath of God, to ask thee then, 'Is there a God now?' I respite thee not till the day of thine own death, when thou shalt have evidence enough, that there is a God, though no other evidence but to find a Devil; and evidence enough, that there is a Heaven, though no other evidence but to feel hell; To ask thee then, 'Is there a God now?' I respite thee but a few hours, but six hours, but till midnight. Wake then: and then, darke and alone, Hear God ask thee then, remember that I asked thee now, 'Is there a God?' and if thou darest, say 'No.'

This sermon is a good example of the rhetorical method of seventeenth-century English divines, in whose best sermons the emotional effect is always the natural product of a reasoned analytical process which never lets go of the feelings of the hearers. But the personal directness and closeness of the climax, as well as the great verbal beauty, of this sermon, are peculiarly Donne's. The reader has the feeling—how much more must the listener have had it—that the preacher is totally identifying himself with the atheist's resistance to God which, by mercilessly and logically analysing it, he succeeds in revealing as a terror and an emptiness: at the climax, we feel that the atheist, lying alone, in his darkened room, cannot escape God because he cannot escape God's word, which reverberates through his head as though the preacher were continuing to haunt him. Nothing could be more dramatically effective than this emotional participation: and yet every step of the way is closely reasoned, so that at no point can the perplexed soul escape the climax save by cutting

N

the labyrinthine knot for a total surrender. The text, the statement, is explained, examples are quoted, and the hearer is led from premises his reason cannot deny to conclusions which, though reason might not have foreseen them (that, after all, is the preacher's job), yet neither reason nor feeling can escape. Donne sinks all his own experience and all his imagination into his final, unashamedly emotional appeal. For the preacher's aim was to capture and then exploit the feelings of his listeners, so there must be logic—a man will not convince others who cannot demonstrate the logic of his own conviction; once the attention has been captured, every device of rhetoric is brought into play to hold that attention and work upon it. 'Knowledge cannot save us, but we cannot be saved without knowledge.'

In a sermon preached on Christmas Day, 1621, Donne speaks at length of the place of reason in the scheme of faith.

The reason therefore of man must first be satisfied, but the way of such satisfaction must be this, to make him see, that this World, a frame of so much harmony, so much concinnitie and conveniencie, and such a correspondence and subordination in the parts thereof, must necessarily have had a workman, for nothing can make itself. . . Knowledge cannot save us, but we cannot be saved without knowledge; Faith is not on this side knowledge, but beyond it, we must necessarily come to knowledge first, though we must not stay at it when we are come thither. For a regenerate Christian, being now a new creature, hath also a new facultie of reason, and so believeth the mysteries of religion out of another Reason, then as a mere natural man he believed naturall and morall things. He believeth them for their own sake, by Faith, though he take knowledge of them before, by that common reason and by those humane arguments which work upon other men in naturall or morall things. Divers men may walke by the seaside, and the same beams of the sun giving light to them all, one gathereth by the benefit of that light pebbles or speckled shells for curious vanitie; and another gathers precious Pearl or medicinal amber, by the same light. So the common light of reason illumines us all; but one employs this light upon the searching of impertinent vanities, another by a better use of the same light finds out the mysteries of religion; and when he hath found them, loves them, not for the light's sake, but for the natural and true worth of the thing itself.

In this beautiful and characteristic image of light, Donne shows that for him religion dwelt in the clarity of reason and not merely in the darkness of despair. The charnel-house and the graveyard sides of Donne's religion have been much exaggerated. There are those aspects: and no one can make the flesh creep, in the authentic Jacobean manner, better than Donne when he wishes his hearers to look to their end. When he preaches of death, he speaks of an old personal enemy-friend, with a sense of horror which he was certainly the greater preacher for never having quite exorcized: but in his sombre sermons on death and hell there is nothing of relish. The most famous example is of course his last sermon, 'Death's Duell', which so took the imagination of those who heard it, with its terrifying 'This whole world is but an universall churchyard, but our common grave'. . . . Equally powerful is the great sermon on mortality which he preached on 8 March 1622 '. . . when everlasting darkness shall have an inchoation in the present dimness of mine eyes, and the everlasting gnashing in the present chattering of my teeth, and the everlasting worme in the present gnawing of the agonies of my body and anguishes of my mind . . . ', a sermon whose merit Coleridge admitted, though he added that 'it is too much in the style of the monkish preachers,

Papam redolat' [it stinks of Popery]. Yet these celebrated passages can be matched with as many in which light prevails:

[On heaven] . . . 'where we shall end, and yet begin but then; where we shall have continual rest and yet never grow lazy; where we shall be stronger to resist, and yet have no enemy; where we shall live and never die, where we shall meet and never part'.

'*Et in finem*, he loved them to the end. It is much that he should love them *in fine*, at their end, that he should look graciously at last; that when their sun sets, their eyes faint, his sun of grace should arise and his east should be brought to their west . . .' (here again is the familiar and favourite geographical metaphor).

'Joy is peace for having done that which we ought to have done. . . . To have something to do, to do it, and then to rejoice in having done it, to embrace a calling, to perform the duties of that calling, to joy and rest in the peaceful testimony of having done so; this is Christianly done, Christ did it. . . .'

'I shall rise from the dead, from the dark station, from the prostration, from the prosternation of death, and never misse the sun which shall then be put out, for I shall see the sonne of God, the sunne of glory, and shine myself as that sunne shines.'

In the last of those four passages, the phrase 'dark station' is characteristically multiplied according to rhetorical principles, involving repetition of meaning, assonance and progressive elaboration. If a modern writer had hit on the phrase, he would have written only 'I shall rise from the dead, from the dark station of death'.

A good example of rhetorical elaboration in parallels (one side of the 'parallel' being man) occurs in a sermon[1]

---

[1] Sermon LXXII in the 1640 collection.

first preached at The Hague in 1619. The initial proposition states both sides of the comparison in a familiar
image: 'The world is a sea in many respects and assimila-
tions.' Some of those are then given: the sea's depth and
power to destroy are the same in storm as in calm
weather: i.e. the world can destroy a man in prosperity
or in adversity. The sea is 'bottomless to any line': i.e.
the purpose of the world is inscrutable. Men are subject to ebbs and floods of health and fortune, as the sea is
to the tides. 'All these ways,' says Donne, 'the world is
a sea, but especially it is a sea in this respect, that the sea
is no place of habitation, but a passage to our habitations.'
Here Donne, like any Elizabethan or Jacobean writer, is
on familiar ground (or rather water): the image is a
natural one for an island-dweller.

The rhetorical method is the method of all medieval
and Renaissance prose written to persuade rather than
simply to entertain, particularly, of course, theological
prose. A theme, a topic, a biblical truth alike yield
their secrets upon the application of examples drawn
from various fields of learning and experience: and all
secular studies, all human experiences, were handmaids
to Divinity, Queen of sciences and arts. Thus, in this
particular sermon Donne is able, under the general
proposition 'the world is a sea,' to subsume the Christian
image 'we are fishers of men' with that accuracy of
parallel demanded by the spirit and technique of the age.
'Eloquence is not our net, Traditions of men are not
our nets, only the Gospel is. The devil angles with hooks
and bayts . . . the Gospel of Christ Jesus is a net, it hath
leads and corks. It hath leads, that is the denouncing
of God's judgments, and a power to sink down and lay
flat any stubborne and rebellious heart; and it hath
corkes, that is, the power of absolution and application
of the mercies of God, that swimme above all his workes,

meanes to erect an humble and contrite spirit above all the waters of tribulation. . . .' The complete theologian must be a compleat angler as well as a psychologist, philosopher, lawyer, doctor and logician. It is to be hoped that this passage gave an appropriate pleasure to Donne's first biographer.

In another sermon, Donne used the analogy of fishing in a still more original way. 'The rebuke of sin, is like the fishing of *whales*; the marke is great enough one can scarce miss hitting. But if there be not *sea room* and line enough, and a dexterity in letting out that line, he that hath fixed his harping iron in the whale, endangers himself and his boate. God hath made us fishers of men, and when we have struck a whale, touched the conscience of any person . . . it [the guilty conscience] struggles and strives and as much as it can, endeavours to draw fishers and boate, the Man and his fortune, into contempt and danger. But if God tie a sickness or any other calamity to the end of the line, that will winde up this whale again, to the boate, bring back this rebellious sinner better advised, to the mouth of the minister for more counsell. . . .'

Such imagery, drawn from secular life, captures our attention today much as those vivid homely marginal illustrations of secular life in the Luttrell Psalter capture the attention of someone for whom the main religious text has little to offer. Perhaps, when the sermon was first preached, it had the same effect on some who were curious about whales but incurious about God, persuading them that because analogy was possible, because identification helped, because all secular arts and sciences could become instruments of religious truth, therefore that truth was not remote or difficult or meaningless but belonged to everyone's life. In an interesting sermon, on Psalm 55, 19: *Because they have no changes, therefore they fear not God,* Donne speaks of how we come to sin 'upon reason, and upon discourse, upon Meditation and upon plot, This is *humanum*, to become the man of sin, to surrender that which is the form and essence of man, Reason and understanding, to the service of sin'. Having put reason to the service of sin, we 'shall come to sin through all the arts and all our knowledge, to sin grammatically, to tie sins together in construction . . . and coherence upon one another: And to sin Historically, to sin over sins of other men again, to sin by precedent . . . and we come to sin Rhetorically, persuasively, powerfully'. Because Donne could understand so well the Renaissance love of know-ledge, sense of adventure, capacity for discovery in the physical and intellectual worlds, he could speak, without leaving the literal truth, of men sinning through all the arts and through all knowledge. To sin is to live in a way which is natural to man as a fallen creature, and which, therefore, is bound to exercise all the faculties of the sinner. So the priest must combat sin with all the arts and with all his knowledge, showing how the same tools may be put at the service of God as are now put at the service of sin. Because we sin grammatically, syntactically, the preacher must use all the arts of logic to direct our emotions and thoughts towards the possi-bility and the logic of goodness. Because we sin histori-cally, the preacher must be an historian and show us that God also is in history. Because we sin 'rhetorically, persuasively, powerfully', the preacher must speak rhetorically, persuasively and powerfully to gain his point and do his work.

'Dr. Donne', wrote Coleridge in his *Notes on English Divines*, 'was an eminently witty man in a very witty age, but to the honour of his judgment let it be said, that though his great wit is evinced in numberless passages, in a few only is it shown off.' This is on the whole true of Donne's sermons, in which his wit is only rarely shown off. Indeed, he has himself been sufficiently severe upon sheer showing-off in one of his sermons, where he might well be thinking of his own early love-poems: 'For howsoever some men out of a petulancy and wantonness of wit have called the faculties and abilities of woman in question, even in the root thereof, in the reasonable and immortal soul . . . no author of gravity . . . could admit that doubt, whether women were created in the image of God, that is in possession of a reasonable and immortal soul.' Donne was now an author of gravity, and a preacher in earnest. Yet he did not, thanks to the genius of his age, cease to be, in the truest, gravest and most earnest definition of wit, a very witty man: in his best sermons all things agree, without either discord or confusion.

It is certainly not a petulancy and wantonness of wit that makes Donne's sermons difficult for a modern reader. The difficulty arises from the fact that most of the time he is concerned with theological ideas and expositions of dogmatic truth which are no longer a part of our own thought. In addition, there is a good deal of sales-resistance to the sermon as such: we do not nowadays associate it with literature, and it does not nowadays have much reason to expect such an association. Fortunately, however, the most beautiful and eloquent passages in Donne's sermons are those in which he speaks, not words of indoctrination but 'comfortable words', in which his subject is those secret longings, fears and dreams which humanity has not yet outgrown. The whole vast elaborate machinery of medieval theology has, after all, a lowest common denominator: from Augustine to Aquinas, Catholicism wore at her heart the idealism of Plato, the 'melancholy optimism', as

Bertrand Russell calls it, of Plotinus. Nowadays, Christianity is practical and unplatonic. To Donne, though it had its practical side, it was primarily ideal, a means of understanding the whole of creation. He was not an original philosopher nor a mystic; he saw heaven and earth in the traditional way. 'He that asks me what heaven is, means not to hear me but to silence me, for he knows I cannot tell him,' he said, for he knew that as a theologian he could but expound the attributes of the ineffable, describing the next world in terms of his experience of this world, and proclaiming man's need for God as a personal testimony. 'All the world', he said in one of his sermons, 'is but *speculum*, a glasse, in which we see God.'

As a poet, Donne had often indulged in fantastic and peculiar comparisons of macrocosm and microcosm, had often shattered the mirror into many original images. But in the end, it is the mirror itself, the profoundly sober, orthodox and unoriginal summing-up, which perhaps matters least to us, that would have mattered most to him. For the particular can be wrong, and may 'perish for want of being understood', but the universal, the general and the ideal remain. We, in a non-theological, non-ideal and empirical age, have reversed this valuation and read Donne, as we can, as the monarch of wit, although he himself asked 'what is any monarch to the whole world? and the whole world is but that: but what? but nothing'.

SELECT BIBLIOGRAPHY

A. *Texts*

POEMS OF JOHN DONNE, edited by Sir H. Grierson (complete text with introduction and notes: 2 vols., 1912).

POEMS OF JOHN DONNE, edited by Sir H. Grierson (one-volume edition, Oxford Standard Authors: 1933).

COMPLETE POETRY AND SELECTED PROSE, edited by John Hayward ('Nonesuch' Donne: 1929).

JOHN DONNE: THE DIVINE POEMS, edited by Helen Gardner (text, introduction and notes: 1953).

THE ELEGIES, AND THE SONGS AND SONNETS, edited by Helen Gardner (1965).

JOHN DONNE: THE SATIRES, EPIGRAMS AND VERSE LETTERS, edited by W. Milgate (1967).

SELECTED PROSE, edited by E. M. Simpson, Helen Gardner, and T. Healy (1967).

SERMONS OF JOHN DONNE IN TEN VOLUMES, edited by G. R. Potter and E. M. Simpson (1953–1962).

DEVOTIONS, edited by J. Sparrow (1923).

PARADOXES AND PROBLEMS, edited by G. Keynes (1923).

ESSAYS IN DIVINITY, edited by E. M. Simpson (1952).

METAPHYSICAL LYRICS AND POEMS OF THE SEVENTEENTH CENTURY, edited by Sir. H Grierson (with introductory essay: 1921).

THE METAPHYSICAL POETS, edited by Helen Gardner (with introductory essay: 1959).

B. *Biographical and Critical*

LIFE, by Izaak Walton (World's Classics, 1927).

LIFE AND LETTERS OF JOHN DONNE, by Sir E. Gosse (2 vols., 1899).

'ABRAHAM COWLEY' in LIVES OF THE POETS, by Samuel Johnson (World's Classics, 1906).

'THE METAPHYSICAL POETS' and 'ANDREW MARVELL', by T. S.
   Eliot (1921). Both printed in *Selected Essays* (1932).
REVALUATION, by F. R. Leavis (1936).
THE MONARCH OF WIT, by J. B. Leishman (1951).
DONNE AND THE DRURYS, by R. C. Bald (1959).
THE PROSE WORKS OF JOHN DONNE, by E. M. Simpson (1948).
JOHN DONNE: TWENTIETH CENTURY VIEWS, edited by Helen
   Gardner (Prentice-Hall, 1962).
JOHN DONNE, PETRARCHIST, by D. L. Guss (1966).
THE POETRY OF MEDITATION, by L. L. Martz (1962).

C. *Articles*

For review-articles on Helen Gardner's text of *The Elegies, and
the Songs and Sonnets*, see W. Empson, in *Critical Quarterly*, VIII
(1966), pp. 255–280; and M. Roberts in *Essays in Criticism*,
XVI (1966), pp. 309–329.

'TWO NOTES ON DONNE', by E. M. Simpson, in *Review of
   English Studies* (new series), XVI (1965), pp. 140–150.
'DONNE'S *Epithalamium made at Lincoln's Inn*', by D. Novarr, in
   Review of English Studies (new series), VII (1956), pp. 250–
   263.
'THE METAPHYSIC OF LOVE', by A. J. Smith, in *Review of English
   Studies* (new series), IX (1958), pp. 362–375.
'SOME OF DONNE'S ECSTASIES', by Merritt Y. Hughes, in *PMLA*,
   75 (1960), pp. 509–518.
'TWO DONNE POEMS', by I. A. Shapiro, in *Times Literary
   Supplement*, 9 April, 1949, p. 233.

INDEX

195